God Bless You on Your Confirmation Day

October 29, 2017

From Saint Paul
Lutheran Church

and

The Women of Saint Paul
Lutheran Church (WELCA)

God's Little Devotional Book
for Teens

God's Little Devotional Book
for Teens

David C Cook
transforming lives together

GOD'S LITTLE DEVOTIONAL BOOK FOR TEENS
Published by David C Cook
4050 Lee Vance View
Colorado Springs, CO 80918 U.S.A.

David C Cook Distribution Canada
55 Woodslee Avenue, Paris, Ontario, Canada N3L 3E5

David C Cook U.K., Kingsway Communications
Eastbourne, East Sussex BN23 6NT, England

The graphic circle C logo is a registered trademark of David C Cook.

Unless otherwise indicated, all Scripture quotations are taken from the King
James Version of the Bible. (Public Domain.) Scripture quotations marked NIV
are taken from the *New International Version*®. *NIV*®. Copyright © 1973, 1978,
1984 by International Bible Society. Used by permission of Zondervan. All rights
reserved; TLB are taken from *The Living Bible*, © 1971, Tyndale House Publishers,
Wheaton, IL 60189. Used by permission; NASB are taken from the *New American
Standard Bible*, © Copyright 1960, 1995 by The Lockman Foundation. Used by
permission; and AB are taken from *The Amplified Bible*. Copyright © 1954, 1958,
1962, 1964, 1965, 1987 by The Lockman Foundation. Used by permission.

ISBN 978-1-56292-211-5
eISBN 978-1-4347-0481-8

© 1991 David C Cook

Designed by Koechel Peterson & Associates
Cover Photos: © istockphoto.com

Printed in the United States of America
First Edition 1991

13 14 15 16

121015

Introduction

You're not yet an adult, but you're not really a kid anymore, either. You may be twelve or thirteen and just beginning the teen years; fifteen or sixteen and about to get your driver's license; or seventeen or eighteen and about to graduate from high school. These are the years someone once called the "tween" years.

In today's high-pressure, fast-paced world, it's not easy being a teenager. You're faced with difficult situations every day. Friends and peers may pressure you to do things you don't want to do. They may pressure you to do things you think you might want to do but know you shouldn't. What you need is the strength, resolve, and encouragement to pass up those temporarily enticing and exciting things in order to work toward God's destiny for your life.

God does have a plan for your life. His plan is a good one. He has a plan for you to prosper. His plan will give you hope and a bright future. (See Jeremiah 29:11.)

God's Little Devotional Book for Teens was designed to encourage and inspire you to discover, desire, and implement God's divine plan for your life. The powerful quotes and Scriptures will give you something on which to meditate, and the devotional stories will help you to apply their principles. Is life challenging? Sure . . . but with God's help and guidance, your future is great!

When you were born, you cried and the world rejoiced. Live your life in such a manner that when you die the world cries and you rejoice.

A painting in an ancient temple depicts a king forging a chain from his crown, and nearby, another scene shows a slave converting his chain into a crown. Underneath the painting is this inscription: "Life is what one makes it, no matter of what it is made."

You may have been born with certain ingredients, just as a baker may find the staples of flour, sugar, and oil in his kitchen; but what you create from the talents and abilities God has given you is up to you! Live your life so that it might be measured according to these words of an anonymous poet:

> Not—How did he die? But—How did he live?

Not—What did he gain? But—What
did he give?
These are the units to measure the worth
Of a man as a man, regardless of birth.
Not—What was his station? But—had
he a heart?
And—How did he play his God-given
part?
Was he ever ready with a word of
good cheer,
To bring back a smile, to banish a tear?
Not—What was his shrine? Nor—
What was his creed?
But—Had he befriended those really
in need?
Not—What did the sketch in the
newspaper say?
But—How many were sorry when he
passed away?

• •

The memory of the righteous will be a blessing.

PROVERBS 10:7 NIV

Many receive advice;
only the wise profit by it.

After arguing heatedly for several hours about which type of water main to purchase for their city, the town council of Pacific Vista was still deadlocked. One member suggested, "Let's appoint a committee to confer with the city engineer at Los Angeles to find out which type they have found to be most successful over the years. If we can profit by another city's mistakes, I think we should do so."

Leaping to his feet, an angry councilman—obviously full of civic pride but with little discretion—replied, pounding his fist on the table, "Why should we have to profit by the mistakes of Los Angeles? Gentlemen, I contend that Pacific Vista is a big enough town now to make its own mistakes!"

Most of us are surrounded by good advice at any given time.

- The books in our libraries are full of it.
- Pastors proclaim it weekly.
- People with highly varied experiences and backgrounds abound with it.
- Schools give access to it; labs report it.
- Commentators and columnists gush with it.

All the good advice in the world is worth very little if it is ignored. Be one of the wise—value and apply the advice you receive.

• •

Pride only breeds quarrels, but wisdom
is found in those who take advice.

PROVERBS 13:10 NIV

> The only way to have
> a friend is to be one.

Mary Lennox "was not an affectionate child and had never cared much for anyone;" and no wonder. Ignored by her parents and raised by servants, she had no concept of what life was like outside of India. Other children called her "Mistress Mary Quite Contrary," because she didn't like to share and always insisted on having her own way.

When Mary was nine years old, her parents died of cholera, and she was sent to live at her uncle's home in England. The move did nothing to improve her disposition. She expected anyone and everyone to jump when she snapped her fingers.

Gradually, however, Mary began to change. Realizing how lonely she was, she asked a robin in the garden to be her friend. She began treating her maid with more respect. Won over by the guilelessness of her maid's little brother, Dickon, and craving his approval, Mary found herself seeking his advice. She even revealed to him the location of her secret garden. Eventually, Mary convinced her crippled cousin, Colin, to grab hold of life with both hands. By the last page of *The Secret Garden*, Mary's transformation is complete. She is happy with herself and surrounded by friends.

To make a friend, you first must make a choice to become a friend.

• •

A man that hath friends
must shew himself friendly.

PROVERBS 18:24

The world wants your best, but God wants your all.

In *The Great Divorce*, C.S. Lewis tells the story of a ghost who carries a little red lizard on his shoulder. The lizard constantly twitches its tail and whispers to the ghost, who all the while urges it to be quiet. When a bright and shining presence appears and offers to rid the ghost of his troublesome baggage, the ghost refuses. He realizes that to quiet the beast, it is necessary to kill it.

A series of rationalizations begins. The ghost reasons that perhaps the lizard need not die but instead might be trained, suppressed, put to sleep, or gradually removed. The shining presence responds that the only recourse is all or nothing.

Finally, the ghost gives permission for the presence to twist the lizard away from him. The presence breaks the lizard's back as he flings it to the ground. In that moment, the ghost becomes a flesh-and-blood man, and the lizard becomes a beautiful gold-and-silver stallion, a creature of power and beauty. The man leaps onto the great horse, and they ride into the sunrise as one.

Lewis concludes by saying, "What is a lizard compared with a stallion? Lust is a poor, weak, whimpering, whispering thing compared with that richness and energy of desire which will arise when lust has been killed."

• •

Thou shalt love the Lord thy God
with all thy heart, and with all
thy soul, and with all thy mind.

MATTHEW 22:37

When you give God your all,
you put yourself in a
position to receive His all.

The story is told of a small dog that was struck by a car and tossed to the edge of the road. A doctor, who just happened to be driving by, noticed that the dog was still alive, so he stopped his car, picked up the dog, and took him home with him. He discovered the dog had suffered only a few minor cuts and abrasions. Reviving the dog, the doctor cleaned its wounds, then carried it to the garage, where he intended to provide a temporary bed.

The dog wriggled free from his arms, however, jumped to the ground, and scampered off. "What an ungrateful dog," the doctor said to himself. He was glad that the dog had recovered so quickly, but was a little miffed that the dog had shown so little appreciation for his expert, gentle care.

He thought no more about the incident until the next evening, when he heard a scratching at his front door. When he opened the door, he found the little dog he had treated. At its side was another injured dog!

Be encouraged! You may never see the difference you make in someone's life or the difference that person will make in the lives of others; nevertheless, those with whom you share the Gospel will *never* be the same.

• •

Go ye into all the world, and preach
the gospel to every creature.

MARK 16:15

> No horse gets anywhere until
> he is harnessed. No life ever
> grows great until it is
> focused, dedicated, disciplined.

Charles Oakley, forward for the New York Knicks and an NBA All-Star, has a reputation for being one of basketball's best rebounders. It's his toughness, however, that has probably contributed the most to his outstanding sports career.

While other professional players seem to have frequent injuries or are sidelined for other reasons, Oakley has had very few injuries over the course of his thirteen-year career, even though he has absorbed a great deal of physical punishment on the court. He is often pushed and fouled. He puts in miles each game running up and down the court. He frequently dives into the stands for loose balls, to the extent that the courtside media teases him about being a working hazard.

According to Oakley, his tenacity and energy have an origin: his grandfather, Julius Moss.

Moss was a farmer in Alabama who did most of his field work by hand. "Other people had more equipment than he did," Oakley says. "He didn't have a tractor, but he got the work done. No excuses." Moss, who died in 1990, developed all sorts of aches and pains in his life, but he laughed at them and went about his business. Oakley saw a lesson in that—nothing should prevent him from earning a day's pay.

Being focused, dedicated, and disciplined will make the difference between a mediocre life and a *great* life.

• •

In a race everyone runs but only one person
gets first prize. . . . To win the contest
you must deny yourselves many things
that would keep you from doing your best.

1 CORINTHIANS 9:24–25 TLB

I have never been hurt
by anything I didn't say.

A young attorney, just out of law school and beginning his first day on the job, sat down in the comfort of his brand-new office with a great sigh of satisfaction. He had worked long and hard to savor such a moment. Then, noticing a prospective client coming toward his door, he began to look busy and energetic. Opening his legal pad and uncapping his pen, he picked up the telephone, and cradling it under his chin, he began to write furiously as he said, "Look, Harry, about that amalgamation deal. I think I better run down to the factory and handle it personally. Yes. No. I don't think three million dollars will swing it. We better have Smith from Los Angeles meet us there. Okay. Call you back later."

Hanging up the phone, he put down his pen, looked up at his visitor, stood, extended his hand, and said in his most polite but confident attorney's voice, "Good morning. How might I help you?"

The prospective client replied, "Actually, I'm just here to hook up your phone."

Many a foible or flaw
Need not show . . . for
If you don't say so,
Others won't know!

There's an old saying that goes, "A shut mouth gathers no foot." Sometimes the best thing to do is just keep your mouth shut!

• •

Don't talk so much. You keep
putting your foot in your mouth.
Be sensible and turn off the flow!

PROVERBS 10:19 TLB

. . . .

We too often love things and use
people, when we should be
using things and loving people.

. . . .

One day, a boy at summer camp received a
box of cookies from his mother. He ate a few,
then placed the box under his bed. The next day,
he discovered the cookies were gone. Later, a
counselor who had been told of the theft saw a
boy sitting behind a tree, eating the stolen
cookies. He sought out the victim and said, "Bill,
I know who stole your cookies. Will you help me
teach him a lesson?" The boy replied, "Well, I
guess—but aren't you going to punish him?"

The counselor said, "Not directly—that
would only make him hate you. I have an idea;
but first I want you to ask your mother to send
some more cookies." The boy did as the counselor asked, and a few days later, another box of
cookies arrived.

The counselor then said, "The boy who stole your cookies is by the lake. I suggest you go down there and share your cookies with him." The boy protested, "But he's the one who stole the first ones from me!" "I know," said the counselor. "Let's see what happens."

An hour later, the counselor saw the boys coming up the hill—the thief earnestly trying to get his new friend to accept his compass in payment for the stolen cookies, and the victim just as adamantly refusing, saying that a few old cookies didn't matter all that much!

Often the best way to get back at someone is to show them God's love. You can usually make a friend in the process.

• •

Be devoted to one another in brotherly love.

Honor one another above yourselves.

ROMANS 12:10 NIV

When you flee temptations,
don't leave a forwarding address.

Velazquez Polk and Janet Kuzmaak both
grew up in Portland, Oregon, but the two could
not have been more different. Polk was a tough
street kid who joined a gang at age ten and was
eventually arrested for selling drugs.

Kuzmaak was an honor roll student from an
upper-class neighborhood. In 1980, Kuzmaak's
sister was raped and strangled to death.
Authorities never found her killer. She came to
regard every criminal as her sister's murderer.

Kuzmaak eventually became a nurse at a
major medical center. Polk, released from jail in
1990, was given a job as her surgical aide.
Kuzmaak was furious. She didn't believe in reha-
bilitation for criminals, but she noticed that when
Polk's gang-member friends tried to entice him to
rejoin their ranks, he refused. He told Kuzmaak

he wanted to flee his old life and join a program to become a nurse's aide. She remembered that her sister had once befriended a man on parole, so she lobbied the hospital to pay Polk's tuition while she continued to monitor him.

Today, she and Polk are great friends. She helped him gain entrance into a world that he once did not know existed. He helped sweep away the bitterness that had once poisoned her heart.

Change and growth are always possible if you first turn away from evil, determined not to return.

• •

Now flee from youthful lusts and
pursue righteousness ... with those
who call on the Lord from a pure heart.

2 TIMOTHY 2:22 NASB

Whatever you dislike in
another person, take care
to correct in yourself.

In *A Closer Walk,* Catherine Marshall
writes: "One morning last week He gave me an
assignment: for one day I was to go on a 'fast'
from criticism. I was not to criticize anybody
about anything."

"For the first half of the day, I simply felt a
void, almost as if I had been wiped out as a
person. This was especially true at lunch. . . . I listened to the others and kept silent. . . . In our talk-
ative family no one seemed to notice. Bemused, I
noticed that my comments were not missed. The
federal government, the judicial system, and the
institutional church could apparently get along
fine without my penetrating observations. But still
I didn't see what this fast on criticism was accom-
plishing—until midafternoon."

"That afternoon, a specific, positive vision for this life was dropped into my mind with God's unmistakable hallmark on it—joy! Ideas began to flow in a way I had not experienced in years. Now it was apparent what the Lord wanted me to see. My critical nature had not corrected a single one of the multitudinous things I found fault with. What it had done was to stifle my own creativity."

Before you are tempted to criticize someone, examine your own life. While you may not commit the same act or have the same habit you're about to criticize, you probably have some behavior that *could* be criticized. Don't stifle your creativity with criticism!

• •

"Why do you look at the speck of sawdust in your brother's eye and pay no attention to the plank in your own eye?"

MATTHEW 7:3 NIV

Shoot for the moon. Even if you miss it you will land among the stars.

A young man who was confused about his future and in a quandary as to which direction to take with his life sat in a park, watching squirrels scamper among the trees. Suddenly, a squirrel jumped from one high tree to another. It appeared to be aiming for a limb so far out of reach that the leap looked like suicide. As the young man had anticipated, the squirrel missed its mark; but it landed, safe and unconcerned, on a branch several feet lower. Then it climbed to its goal, and all was well.

An old man sitting on the other end of the bench remarked, "Funny, I've seen hundreds of 'em jump like that, especially when there are dogs all around and they can't come down to the ground. A lot of 'em miss, but I've never seen any hurt in trying." Then he chuckled and added, "I guess they've got to risk it if they don't want to spend their whole life in one tree."

The young man thought, *A squirrel takes a chance. Do I have less nerve than a squirrel?* He made up his mind in that moment to take the risk he had been thinking about. Sure enough, he landed safely, in a position higher than he had even dared to imagine.

What dream are you aiming for? Does it seem out of reach? Take a leap of faith. God will always catch you if you fall.

• •

Aim for perfection.

2 CORINTHIANS 13:11 NIV

• •

The secret of success is to do the
common things uncommonly well.

• •

Helping the deaf to communicate was
Alexander Graham Bell's motivation for his life's
work, perhaps because his mother and wife were
both deaf. "If I can make a deaf-mute talk," Bell
said, "I can make metal talk." For five frustrating
and impoverished years, he experimented with a
variety of materials in an effort to make a metal
disk that, vibrating in response to sound, could
reproduce those sounds and send them over an
electrified wire.

During a visit to Washington, D.C., he called
on Joseph Henry, a scientist who was a pioneer in
research related to electricity. He presented his
ideas to him and asked his advice: Should he let
someone else perfect the telephone, or should he
do it himself? Henry encouraged him to do it
himself, to which Bell complained that he lacked

the necessary knowledge of electricity. Henry's brief solution was, "Get it."

So Bell studied electricity. A year later when he obtained a patent for the telephone, the officials in the patent office credited him with knowing more about electricity than all the other inventors of his day combined.

Hard work. Study. Hope. Persistence. These are all common things. They are the keys, however, to doing uncommonly well.

• •

Seest thou a man diligent in his business?

he shall stand before kings;

he shall not stand before mean men.

PROVERBS 22:29

Definition of status: Buying something you don't need with money you don't have to impress people you don't like.

Guy de Maupassant's *The Necklace* is the story of a young woman, Mathilde, who desires desperately to be accepted into high society. One day her husband, an ordinary man, is given an invitation to an elegant ball. Mathilde borrows a necklace from a wealthy friend to wear to the occasion. During the course of the evening, she receives many compliments from the aristocracy present. Unfortunately, later that night, she realizes she has lost the necklace.

In order to restore the lost jewelry, Mathilde's husband borrows 36,000 francs, tapping every resource available to him. A look-alike necklace is created, and Mathilde gives it to her friend, without telling her what had happened.

For ten years, the couple slaves to pay back the borrowed francs, each of them working two jobs. They are forced to sell their home and live in a slum. One day after the debt had finally been paid, Mathilde runs into her well-to-do friend. She confesses that the necklace she returned is not the one she borrowed, and she learns that the necklace loaned to her had been made from fake gemstones! The borrowed necklace had been worth less than 500 francs.

Trying to keep up appearances almost always leads to falling flat on your face.

• •

"They do all their deeds to be noticed by men."

MATTHEW 23:5 NASB

> I like the dreams of the future better than the history of the past.

A man once took his three-year-old daughter to an amusement park. It was her first visit to such a place, and she was in awe at the sights and sounds, but mostly she was thrilled at the whirl and whiz of the rides. She begged her dad to let her ride one particular ride, even though it was considered the scariest ride for kids her age.

As she whipped around the corners in her kiddy car, she suddenly wrinkled up her face and let loose with a terrified cry. Her father, who was riding in the car with her, struggled to get her attention. With a big smile, he shouted over the roar of the ride, "This is fun!" When the little girl saw that he was not terrified, she began to laugh. The new experience that was initially terrifying had suddenly become enjoyable. In fact, she insisted on riding the same ride three more times!

What a comfort it is to know that our Heavenly Father will not only ride the new rides in life with us, but the future is never scary to Him. He has good things planned for us. When we look into the future from our perspective, we may become frightened. When we look at the future from God's perspective, we are far more likely to shout, "Let's go! Isn't this going to be fun?"

• •

Remember ye not the former things,

neither consider the things of old.

Behold, I will do a new thing.

ISAIAH 43:18–19

The way to get to the top is to get off your bottom.

One day, in the fall of 1894, Guglielmo retreated to his room on the third floor of his parents' home. He had just spent his entire summer vacation reading books and filling note-books with squiggly diagrams. Now the time had come to *work*.

He rose early every morning. He worked all day and long into the night, to the point that his mother became alarmed. He had never been a robust person, but now he was appallingly thin. His face was drawn, and his eyes were often glazed over with fatigue.

Finally, the day came when he announced his instruments were ready. He invited the family to his room, and pushing a button, he succeeded in ringing a bell on the first floor! While his mother was amazed, his father was not. He saw no use in being able to send a signal so short a distance. So Guglielmo labored on. Little by little, he made changes in his invention, so he could send a signal from one hill to the next and then beyond the hill. Eventually, his invention was perfected, partly by inspiration but mostly by perseverance.

Guglielmo Marconi eventually was hailed as the inventor of wireless telegraphy—the forerunner of the radio. He not only received a Nobel Prize in physics for his efforts, but also a seat in the Italian senate and many honorary degrees and titles.

You can accomplish anything you set your heart on by combining your vision with hard work.

● ●

How long will you lie down, O sluggard?
When will you arise from your sleep?

PROVERBS 6:9 NASB

You are only what you are
when no one is looking.

. . . .

Joe Smith was a loyal carpenter who
worked almost two decades for a successful contractor. The contractor called him into his office
one day and said, "Joe, I'm putting you in charge
of the next house we build. I want you to order
all the materials and oversee the job from the
ground up."

Joe accepted the assignment with great
enthusiasm. He studied the blueprints and
checked every measurement and specification.
Suddenly, he had a thought. *If I'm really in
charge, why couldn't I cut a few corners, use less
expensive materials, and put the extra money in
my pocket? Who will know? Once the house is
painted, it will look great.*

So Joe set about his scheme. He ordered
second-grade lumber and inexpensive concrete,

put in cheap wiring, and cut every corner he could. When the home was finished, the contractor came to see it.

"What a fine job you've done!" he said. "You've been such a faithful carpenter to me all these years that I've decided to show you my gratitude by giving you a gift—this house."

Build well today. You will have to live with the character and reputation you construct.

• •

Not with eye-service, as menpleasers;

but as the servants of Christ,

doing the will of God from the heart.

EPHESIANS 6:6

•••••••••••••••••••••••••••••••

There are times when silence is golden,
other times it is just plain yellow.

•••••••••••••••••••••••••••••••

According to an old fable, three men once decided to engage in the religious practice of absolute silence. They mutually agreed to keep a day of quiet from dawn until the stroke of midnight, at which time a full moon was expected to rise from the horizon. They sat cross-legged for hours, concentrating on the distant horizon, eager for darkness to envelop them.

One of them unwittingly noted, "It's difficult not to say anything at all."

The second one replied, "Quiet. You're speaking during the time of silence!"

The third man sighed and then boasted, "Now I'm the only one who hasn't spoken yet."

A rap singer has updated some of the advice given by the book of Ecclesiastes:

There's a time to speak up and a time to shut up.

There's a time to hunker down and a time to go downtown.

There's a time to talk and a time to walk.

There's a time to be mellow and a time not to be yellow.

Silence can be good, but never if it's the result of raw fear or lack of moral fiber.

• •

To every thing there is a season . . .
a time to keep silence, and a time to speak.

ECCLESIASTES 3:1, 7

• •

A true friend never gets in your way
unless you happen to be going down.

• •

In *Life's Bottom Line,* Richard Exley writes,
"Several weeks ago I was agonizing over a situation in which I had to discipline a man. Though I
felt I had done the right thing, and in the right
way, I still grieved for him. As I was wrestling
with my feelings in prayer, I sensed the Lord
speaking to me and I wrote:

> "My son, power is a dangerous thing,
> and it must always be mitigated with My
> eternal love. I will cause you to feel the
> pain of My discipline even when it is
> toward another. You will feel every sting
> of the lash in your own flesh. You must,
> or in your zealousness you would go too
> far. You will grieve, even as Samuel
> grieved for Saul. Yet I will also make you
> feel the awful pain of their sin, for if you
> do not feel that terrible pain, you will
> draw back from administering the disci-
> pline of the Lord."

Exley concludes, "Confrontation is invariably necessary. A relationship seldom achieves its full potential without it; but it is almost always doomed to failure unless it grows out of a deep trust built on honest communication. . . . It is extremely important to take great care to create a safe place of affirmation and acceptance, where a person can be assured, again and again, of our love. Even then, confrontation will be risky and should be undertaken only after we have carefully prepared our hearts before the Lord."

A true friend cares enough to tell you when you're going the wrong way. Don't be afraid to confront a friend, and be willing to listen when a friend confronts you. It's one reason God gave us friends—to help us grow.

• •

If one falls down, his friend can
help him up. But pity the man who
falls and has no one to help him up!

ECCLESIASTES 4:10 NIV

Every job is a self-portrait
of the person who does it.
Autograph your work with excellence.

Long ago, a band of minstrels lived in a
faraway land. They traveled from town to town,
singing and playing their music in hopes of
making a living, but they had not been doing
well financially. Times were hard, and the
common people had little money to spend on
concerts, even though their fee was small.

The group met one evening to discuss their
plight. "I see no reason for opening tonight," one
said. "It's snowing, and no one will come out on
a night like this." Another said, "I agree. Last
night we performed for just a handful. Even
fewer will come tonight."

The leader of the troupe responded, "I know
you are discouraged. I am too, but we have a
responsibility to those who might come. We will

go on, and we will do the best job of which we are capable. It is not the fault of those who come that others do not. They should not be punished with less than our best."

Heartened by his words, the minstrels gave their best performance ever. After the show, the old man called his troupe to him again. In his hand was a note, handed to him by one of the audience members just before the doors closed behind him. Slowly the man read, "Thank you for a beautiful performance." It was signed simply, "Your King."

Everything you do is performed before your king—the King of Kings. Are all of your words and deeds worthy of His audience?

• •

Daniel was preferred above
the presidents and princes,
because an excellent spirit was in him.

DANIEL 6:3

······························

The best things in life are not free.

······························

For years, Arthur Blessit has carried a six-by-ten-foot, eighty-pound cross on his shoulders through towns and cities around the world. "It blows people's minds," he says. Once he has gained their attention, he finds he has a unique opportunity to share the Gospel.

Blessit first became well known for preaching to the hippies of Hollywood's Sunset Strip. He gained national attention when he undertook a cross-carrying journey—along with four members of his rock group, the Eternal Rush—to Washington, D.C. The 3,500-mile trip took seven months to complete.

As the group traveled, they held rallies. Blessit urged fellow Christians to meet him at the Washington Monument at the end of his trip—but not with empty hands. "Christians need to come and give something," he preached. He asked that people bring or send two gifts for the nation's needy, gifts given openly with both hands. Those who went to the capital to meet him found a third opportunity to give. This gift was to be made with an open heart and an open vein—at a bloodmobile parked on the site.

While the Gospel message is free to all who will receive it, the giving of the Gospel costs, and continues to cost, a great deal!

• •

Ye were not redeemed with corruptible
things, as silver and gold. . . . But with
the precious blood of Christ, as of a lamb
without blemish and without spot.

1 PETER 1:18–19

··

You can lead a boy to college,
but you cannot make him think.

··

At Princeton, Woodrow Wilson was first a teacher and later president of the university. Although he was popular with the students, he did have a reputation for cracking down on students who were not serious in their pursuit of an education.

The mother of one young man who was expelled for cheating made a trip to Princeton to talk with Wilson. She pleaded with him to reinstate her son because of the possible adverse reaction his expulsion would have on her own health and reputation. She told him of an impending operation and said she felt certain she would die if her son were not readmitted. Wilson heard her pleas and then responded, taking a very tough stance, "Madam, you force me to say a hard thing. If I had to choose between your life or my life or anybody's life and the good of this college, I should choose the good of the college."

Failure to study and to apply oneself fully to one's studies is a form of rebellion. The same holds for cheating. Do your best in school. Don't blame a teacher for being too hard on you, when the blame actually lies in your being too easy on yourself. Learn to be a thinker!

• •

It is senseless to pay tuition to educate a rebel who has no heart for truth.

PROVERBS 17:16 TLB

······························

*If a man cannot be a Christian in
the place where he is, he cannot
be a Christian anywhere.*

······························

In an extensive opinion survey, *The Day
America Told the Truth,* James Patterson and
Peter Kim reported some startling findings:

- Only 13% saw all Ten Commandments as
  binding and relevant.
- 91% lied regularly, both at work and home.
- Most workers admitted to goofing off an
  average of seven hours a week.
- About half of the workforce admitted
  they regularly called in sick even when
  they felt well.

When they were asked what they would be
willing to do for $10 million, 25% said they would
abandon their families, 23% would be prostitutes
for a week, and 7% would murder a stranger!

Lest you conclude that the people they surveyed were all ungodly criminals, two other statisticians, Doug Sherman and William Hendricks, found that Christians were almost as likely as unbelievers to do such things as steal from the workplace, falsify their income tax, and selectively obey laws.

To truly claim to be a Christian, a person must do far more than go to church occasionally. He or she must strive to be Christlike 24 hours a day, 365 days a year, in all situations and all circumstances.

• •

Don't work hard only when your master is
watching and then shirk when he isn't looking;
work hard and with gladness all the time,
as though working for Christ, doing
the will of God with all your hearts.

EPHESIANS 6:6–7 TLB

Don't ask God for what
you think is good; ask Him for
what He thinks is good for you.

During a prayer meeting one night, an
elderly woman pleaded, "It really doesn't matter
what You do with us, Lord, just have Your way
with our lives." Adelaide Pollard, a rather well-
known itinerant Bible teacher, overheard her
prayer. At the time, she was deeply discouraged
because she had been unable to raise the money
she needed to go to Africa for missionary service.
She was moved by this woman's sincere request
of God, and when she went home that evening,
she meditated on Jeremiah 18:3–4:

> *Then I went down to the potter's*
> *house, and, behold, he wrought a work on*
> *the wheels. And the vessel that he made of*
> *clay was marred in the hand of the potter:*

so he made it again another vessel, as
seemed good to the potter to make it.

Before retiring, Adelaide took pen in hand and wrote in hymn form her own prayer:

"Have Thine own way, Lord! Have Thine own way! Thou art the potter, I am the clay. Mold me and make me after Thy will, while I am waiting, yielded and still.

"Have Thine own way, Lord! Have Thine own way! Search me, and try me, Master, today! Whiter than snow, Lord, wash me just now, as in Thy presence humbly I bow."

The best way to discover the purpose for your life and how to do it is to give your whole life to God. Then he can fulfill His plan for you.

● ●

After this manner therefore pray ye. . . .

Thy kingdom come. Thy will be

done in earth, as it is in heaven.

MATTHEW 6:9–10

Opportunities are seldom labeled.

In 1970, Wally started baking chocolate chip cookies for his friends, using a recipe and procedure that had been passed down from his aunt Della. For five years, he gave away every batch he made, even though people often told him that his cookies were so good that he should go into business and sell them. Wally had other ideas though. He was determined to become a big-time show-business manager.

Then one day a friend, B.J. Gilmore, told him that she had a friend who could put up the money for a cookie-making business. Her friend never made the investment, but Wally got some of his own friends—including Jeff Wall, Helen Reddy, and Marvin Gaye—to put up some money. Then Wally was off and running.

Originally, he intended to open up only one store on Sunset Boulevard, just enough to make a living. After all, his was the only store in the world dedicated to the sale of nothing but chocolate chip cookies. Business grew virtually overnight. Wally's "Famous Amos Chocolate Chip Cookies" were soon distributed worldwide. Wally himself became a spokesman for other products, from eggs to airlines to a telephone company. While he once dreamed of managing stars, he now is one in his own right!

Sometimes dreams come through the back door. Keep it unlocked!

• •

Seek, and ye shall find; knock, and it shall be opened unto you.

MATTHEW 7:7

•••••••••••••••••••••••••••••••••

The wise does at once
what the fool does at last.

•••••••••••••••••••••••••••••••••

An old legend recounts how Satan once called three of his top aides to a special meeting so that they might make a plan about how to stop the effectiveness of a particular group of Christians. One of the aides, Resentment, proposed, "We should convince them there is no God." Satan sneered at Resentment and replied, "That would never work. They know there's a God."

Bitterness then spoke up: "We'll convince them that God does not really care about right or wrong." Satan thought about the idea for a few moments but then rejected it. "Too many know that God does care," he finally said.

Malice then proposed his idea. "We'll let them go on thinking there is a God and that He cares about right and wrong, but we will keep whispering, 'there is no hurry, there is no hurry, there is no hurry.'"

Satan howled with delight! The plan was adopted, and Malice was promoted to an even higher position in Satan's malevolent hierarchy.

Who can tell how many souls have been lost or lives sorely wounded because someone has held to the commonly acceptable notion: *Delay is okay.*

• •

He that gathereth in summer is
a wise son: but he that sleepeth in
harvest is a son that causeth shame.

PROVERBS 10:5

Nothing great was ever achieved without enthusiasm.

After years of working in Rome on life-size sculptures, Michelangelo went to Florence, where a large block of splendid white Carrara marble had been obtained for a colossal statue. Within weeks, he had signed an agreement to complete a rendition of David for the cathedral. Contract in hand, he started in at once, working with a furious energy so great that he often slept in his clothes, resenting the time it took to take them off and put them on again. He faultlessly examined and precisely measured the marble to see what pose it could accommodate. He made sketches of possible attitudes and careful, detailed drawings from models. He tested his ideas in wax on a small scale. When he was finally satisfied with his design, only then did he pick up a chisel and mallet.

Michelangelo approached painting the ceiling of the Sistine Chapel with the same intensity. He took only a month to develop the theme, then launched with a fury into the final design, building scaffolding, and hiring helpers. Lying at uncomfortable angles on hard boards, breathing the suffocating air just under the vault—plaster dust inflaming his eyes and irritating his skin—he spent much of the next four years literally sweating in physical distress as he worked.

May you do your work with the same passionate enthusiasm!

· ·

The joy of the LORD is your strength.

NEHEMIAH 8:10

· 59 ·

> Trust in yourself and you are
> doomed to disappointment; but
> trust in God, and you are never to
> be confounded in time or eternity.

Marian had her sights set on becoming a concert singer, a challenge that was doubly difficult because of the color of her skin. Her mother, however, had a patient trust in God. Marian later said, "Mother's religion made her believe that she would receive what was right for her to have if she was conscientious in her faith. If it did not come, it was because He had not considered it right for her. We grew in this atmosphere of faith that she created. . . . We believed as she did because we wanted the same kind of haven in the time of storm."

When Marian was denied admission to a famous music conservatory on account of her race, her mother calmly said that "someone would be raised up" to help her accomplish what she had hoped to do at the conservatory. That someone arrived only a few weeks later. One of Philadelphia's most outstanding voice teachers, Guiseppe Boghetti, made room for her to become one of his students.

Marian Anderson was on her way to becoming one of the most magnificent singers of the twentieth century. On Easter Sunday in 1939, she sang for more than 75,000 people gathered in front of the Lincoln Memorial and gave a performance never forgotten by those who were there. Trusting her future to God, she accomplished more than she could have dreamed.

Regardless of the opposition you encounter in reaching your dream, always remember that God is on your side.

• •

It is better to take refuge in
the LORD than to trust in man.

PSALM 118:8 NIV

Don't be discouraged;
everyone who got where
he is, started where he was.

During the late 1960s, a couple was vacationing in the California mountains one day and they noticed a pleasant-appearing young man sitting by a bridge near their hotel. Day after day they saw him sitting in that same spot. At first, they assumed he was fishing, but after taking a closer look, they realized he was doing nothing—just sitting and staring into space. Finally, on the last day of their vacation, they couldn't stand it anymore. They just had to ask: "Why do you sit in that one spot all day, every day?"

He replied with a smile, "I happen to believe in reincarnation. I believe that I have lived many times before and that I will have many lives following this one. So this life I'm sitting out."

In reality, it's impossible for any of us to sit out life. Each day, we are either moving forward or backward, getting stronger or weaker, moving higher or lower. Each of us begins every new day with a fresh opportunity to change tomorrow's starting point.

You only have one chance at it. What will you do today to make your tomorrow better?

• •

Though your beginning was insignificant,

Yet your end will increase greatly.

JOB 8:7 NASB

• •

Maturity doesn't come with age; it comes
with acceptance of responsibility.

• •

A number of definitions of maturity have
been offered by experts, but these are perhaps
among the best understood by the average person:

Maturity is when you not only want to have a
puppy to call your own, but when you remember
on your own to give it food and water every day.

Maturity is when you not only know how to
dress yourself, but you remember to put your
dirty clothes in the laundry hamper after you've
taken them off.

Maturity is when you not only are capable of
using a telephone to call a friend, but when you
know how to keep your calls short so others can
have access to the phone.

Maturity is when you not only are old enough
to stay at home alone, but when you can be trusted
to stay at home and even have friends over.

Maturity is when you are not only old enough to drive the car by yourself, but you pay for the gasoline you use.

Maturity is when you are not only old enough to stay up late, but you are wise enough to go to bed early.

The more you learn to accept responsibility for your life, the more you will grow in maturity. With greater responsibility and maturity comes greater privileges.

• •

When I was a child, I spake as a child,

I understood as a child, I thought

as a child: but when I became a man,

I put away childish things.

1 CORINTHIANS 13:11

The man who wins may have
been counted out several times,
but he didn't hear the referee.

The difference between success and failure
is often the ability to get up just one more time
than you fall down!

Moses easily could have given up. He had an
interrupted childhood and lived with a foster
family. He also had a strong temper, a stammer-
ing tongue, and a criminal record, but when God
called to him, he ultimately said yes.

Joshua had seen the Promised Land and then
been forced to wander in the wilderness for forty
years with cowards who didn't believe, as he did,
that they could conquer their enemies and
possess the land. He could have given up in discouragement, but he was willing to go when God
said to go.

Peter had a hard time making the transition from fisherman to fisher of men. He sank while trying to walk on water, was strongly rebuked by Jesus for trying to tell Him what to do, and denied knowing Jesus in that hour when Jesus needed him most. He easily could have seen himself as a hopeless failure, but when the opportunity came to preach the Gospel before thousands on the Day of Pentecost, he responded.

No matter what you've done, what mistakes you may have made, what errors you may have committed, you're not a failure until you lie down and quit.

• •

Though a righteous man falls
seven times, he rises again.

PROVERBS 24:16 NIV

The happiest people don't necessarily have the best of everything. They just make the best of everything.

A story is told of identical twins: one a hope-filled optimist who often said, "Everything is coming up roses!" and the other, a sad and hopeless pessimist who continually expected the worst to happen. The concerned parents of the twins brought them to a psychologist, hoping he might be able to help them balance their personalities.

The psychologist suggested that on the twins' next birthday, the parents put them in separate rooms to open their gifts. "Give the pessimist the best toys you can afford," the psychologist said, "and give the optimist a box of manure." The parents did as he said.

When they peeked in on the pessimistic twin, they heard him complaining, "I don't like the color of this toy. I'll bet this toy will break! I don't like to play this game. I know someone who has a bigger toy than this!"

Tiptoeing across the corridor, the parents peeked in and saw their optimistic son gleefully throwing manure up in the air. He was giggling as he said, "You can't fool me! Where there's this much manure, there's gotta be a pony!"

How are you looking at life today? As an accident waiting to happen or a blessing about to be received?

• •

I have learned, in whatsoever state I am,
therewith to be content. . . . I can do all things
through Christ which strengtheneth me.

PHILIPPIANS 4:11, 13

A missionary surgeon in one of China's hospitals restored sight to a man who had been nearly blinded by cataracts. A few weeks later, to his great surprise, forty-eight blind men showed up on his hospital's doorstep. They had all come to be cured. Amazingly, these blind men had walked more than 250 miles from a remote area of China to get to the hospital. They had traveled by holding on to a rope chain. Their guide and inspiration was the man who had been cured.

The Christian evangelist, Dr. J. Wilbur Chapman, concluded from his study of the New Testament Gospels that Jesus healed some forty people personally and directly. Of this number, thirty-four were brought to Him by friends or family members, or Jesus was taken to the ailing person by others. Only six of the forty people healed in the Gospels found their way to Jesus, or He to them, *without* someone giving assistance.

In the Gospels, Jesus refers to His followers as "friends." To them, He was the Friend of friends, closer even than a brother. Not only do you become like the friends with whom you associate, but when you choose to hang out with friends who are like Jesus, you will find yourself imitating Him more and more.

• •

Iron sharpeneth iron; so a man sharpeneth
the countenance of his friend.

PROVERBS 27:17

Famous World War II general, George S. Patton Jr., was an avid reader and student of history. He wrote to his son in 1944: "To be a successful soldier, you must know history. Read it objectively. . . . In Sicily I decided as a result of my information, observations, and a sixth sense that I have that the enemy did not have another large scale attack in his system. I bet my shirt on that and I was right." His sixth sense may very well have been formed by thousands of hours of reading history and both biographies and autobiographies.

Historical parallels were constantly on Patton's mind. When he observed the situation in Normandy on July 2, 1944, he immediately wrote Eisenhower that the German Schlieffen Plan of 1914 could be applied. A month later, an operation such as he had described brought about the German defeat in Normandy.

The book that perhaps influenced Patton most was Ardant du Picque's *Battle Studies.* Patton used it to help solve the problem of getting infantry to advance through enemy artillery fire. He recommended it to Eisenhower: "First read *Battle Studies* by Du Pique (you can get a copy at Leavenworth) then put your mind to a solution."

Most of the successful men in the world are avid readers, especially of biographies. If you are interested in being a success in life, immerse yourself in the life stories of successful people. You will learn from their mistakes and failures as well as their successes and triumphs.

• •

All these things happened to them

as examples——as object lessons to us——

to warn us against doing the same things.

1 CORINTHIANS 10:11 TLB

Many men have too much willpower.
It's won't power they lack.

In *Sin, Sex and Self-Control,* Norman Vincent Peale writes: "Martha took the kids away to the mountains for a month, so I was a summer bachelor. And about midway through that month I met a girl, a beautiful girl looking for excitement. She made it clear that I had a green light . . . . so for one weekend I put my conscience in mothballs and arranged a meeting with her for Saturday night.

"I woke up early Saturday morning with a bit of a hangover; I'd played poker until late the night before. I decided to get up, put on my swimming trunks, and take a walk on the beach to clear my head. I took an ax along, because the wreck of an old barge had come ashore down the beach, and there was a lot of tangled rope that was worth salvaging. . . . There was something about the freshness of the morning and the feel of the ax that made me want to keep on swinging it. So I began to chop in earnest."

As he chopped, a strange thing began to happen. He said, "I felt as if I were outside myself, looking at myself through a kind of fog that was gradually clearing. And suddenly I knew that what I had been planning for that evening was so wrong, so out of key with my standards and my loyalties and the innermost me that it was out of the question." He canceled the date.

Have you exercised your "won't" power lately?

● ●

A man without self-control is as defenseless as a city with broken-down walls.

PROVERBS 25:28 TLB

> It's not hard to make decisions when
> you know what your values are.

Marshall Field once offered the following twelve reminders to help a person obtain a sound sense of values:

1. The value of time.
2. The success of perseverance.
3. The pleasure of working.
4. The dignity of simplicity.
5. The worth of character.
6. The power of kindness.
7. The influence of example.
8. The obligation of duty.
9. The wisdom of economy.
10. The virtue of patience.
11. The improvement of talent.
12. The joy of originating.

Can you state the core principles of your value system today? For some, it is likely to be the Ten Commandments. For others, it is the sayings of Jesus.

Solid values are like unblemished, evenly hewn stones. No matter what you build with them, you can be sure that if you follow the basic laws of construction, the structure will be solid and all your decisions will stand firm.

• •

Daniel purposed in his heart
that he would not defile himself.

DANIEL 1:8

Conquer yourself rather than the world.

When you get what you want in
your struggle for self,

   And the world makes you king for a day,

   Just go to a mirror and look at yourself,

   And see what that man has to say.

   For it isn't your father or mother
or wife,

   Whose judgment upon you must pass;

   The fellow whose verdict counts most
in your life,

   Is the one staring back from the glass.

   Some people may think you are a
straight-shooting chum,

   And call you a wonderful guy,

   But the man in the glass says you're
only a bum,

   If you can't look him straight in the eye.

He's the fellow to please, never mind
all the rest,
    For he's with you clear up to the end,
    And you have passed your most dan-
gerous, difficult test,
    If the man in the glass is your friend.
    You may fool the whole world down
your pathway of years,
    And get pats on the back as you pass,
    But your final reward will be
heartache and tears,
    If you've cheated the man in the glass.
                            —Anonymous
Learn to conquer yourself by developing your
self-control, and you'll be able to look yourself
straight in the eye and know you've done your best.

• •

Encourage the young men to be self-controlled.

TITUS 2:6 NIV

I am only one; but still I am one.
I cannot do everything, but
still I can do something; I will not
refuse to do the something I can do.

Jewish physician Boris Kornfeld was impris-
oned in Siberia. There he worked in surgery,
helping both the staff and prisoners. He met a
Christian whose name is unknown, but whose
quiet faith and frequent reciting of the Lord's
Prayer had an impact on Dr. Kornfeld.

One day while repairing the slashed artery of
a guard, Dr. Kornfeld seriously considered sutur-
ing the artery in such a way that the guard would
slowly die of internal bleeding. The violence he
recognized in his own heart appalled him, and he
found himself saying, "Forgive us our sins as we
forgive those who sin against us." Afterward, he
began to refuse to obey various inhumane,
immoral, prison-camp rules. He knew his quiet
rebellion put his life in danger.

One afternoon, he examined a patient who had undergone an operation to remove cancer. He saw in the man's eyes a depth of spiritual misery that moved him with compassion, and he told him his entire story, including a confession of his secret faith. That very night, Dr. Kornfeld was murdered as he slept, but his testimony was not in vain. The patient who had heard his confession became a Christian as a result. He survived the prison camp and went on to tell the world about life in the gulag. That patient was Aleksandr Solzhenitsyn, who became one of the leading Russian writers of the twentieth century. He revealed to the world the horrors of the prison camps and perils of Russian communism.

One person can truly make a difference. There is something you can do, and only you can do it. God created you with a destiny.

• •

Under [Christ's] direction the whole body
is fitted together perfectly, and each part
in its own special way helps the other parts.

EPHESIANS 4:16 TLB

••••••••••••••••••••••••••••••

Politeness goes far,
yet costs nothing.

••••••••••••••••••••••••••••••

In 1865, after General Ulysses S. Grant had moved his occupying army into Shiloh, he ordered a seven o'clock curfew for the city. One distinguished Southern lady, a Mrs. Johnson, was seen walking near the army's downtown headquarters near the curfew time.

General Grant approached her and said, "Mrs. Johnson, it's a little dangerous out there. I am going to ask two of my officers to escort you home."

She replied determinedly, "I won't go."

Grant smiled, went back in to his headquarters, and returned in a few minutes, wearing an overcoat that covered his insignia and rank, and therefore the fact that he was a Northerner.

"May I walk with you, Mrs. Johnson?" he asked.

"Why, yes," Mrs. Johnson replied, nearly blushing. "I'm always glad to have a gentleman as an escort."

Mrs. Johnson would walk with a man she saw as a *gentleman,* even though she would not walk with a Union soldier. Good manners and genuine politeness go a long way toward "covering" many of our faults, mistakes, and differences.

• •

A kind man benefits himself.

PROVERBS 11:17 NIV

We should behave to our
friends as we would wish
our friends to behave to us.

President Harry Truman had a reputation
for having never been sly or disloyal in his life.
He stood by a friend even when he risked public
ridicule for it.

One of Truman's friends from his army days
was Jim Pendergast, whose uncle Tom was the
head of the Democratic Party in Kansas City. Jim
and his dad urged Truman to run for office—a
judgeship in rural Jackson County. A year later
Truman did so, and with Pendergast's support, he
won the election. As judge, he didn't always agree
with Pendergast's practices. Tom once said to a
group of contractors who had asked him to influence Truman, "I told you he was the hardhead-
edest, orneriest man in the world; there isn't
anything I can do."

Unfortunately, Pendergast's penchant for horse races caused him to be investigated for income tax evasion. He confessed, was fined, and was sentenced to serve fifteen months in a federal penitentiary. When Pendergast died during Truman's vice presidency, Truman didn't hesitate to fly to Kansas City for the funeral. "He was always my friend," Truman said of him, "and I have always been his."

True friendship is not based on what a friend does for you, but on what he means to you.

• •

As ye would that men should do
to you, do ye also to them likewise.

LUKE 6:31

Who ceases to be a friend,
never was one.

In *Lessons from Mom,* Joan Aho Ryan writes about loyalty in friendship. She says, "We went to one of the local shopping malls recently where Mom ran into two women who live in her development. . . . They greeted her effusively. It was a brief exchange, during which she introduced me, and they were on their way. 'What phony baloney,' she said when they were well ahead of us. Since her remark came from nowhere, I asked her what she meant.

"With obvious disdain, she explained that she had sat under the canopy at her pool on several occasions with these two women and one of their friends, Sylvia. One day, she said, she sat nearby and heard the three of them talking about the wedding reception of Sylvia's daughter the week before. They raved about the food, the flowers, the elegant country club location, the beautiful bride. . . . Mom said Sylvia was obviously beaming with pride.

"'Well, then Sylvia left, and you should have heard them,' Mom said. . . . 'I couldn't believe friends could be that two-faced. They ripped her apart, talking about how cheap she was, her homely son-in-law, the music they couldn't dance to. It was awful. And they call themselves friends,' she clucked. 'Who needs friends like that?'"

Speaking well of others is not only a good way to acquire friends, but to keep them.

• •

"'These people honor me with their lips,
but their hearts are far from me.'"

MARK 7:6 NIV

Have you ever watched an icicle form? Did you notice how the dripping water froze, one drop at a time, until the icicle was a foot long or more?

If the water was clean, the icicle remained clear and sparkled brightly in the sun; but if the water was slightly muddy, the icicle looked cloudy, its beauty spoiled.

Our character is formed in the same way. Each thought or feeling adds its layer of influence. Each decision we make—about matters both great and small—contributes. Every outside influence that we take into our minds and souls—be they impressions, experiences, visual images, or the words of others—helps build our character.

We must remain concerned at all times about the droplets that we allow to drip into our lives. Just as habits born of hate, falsehood, and evil intent mar and eventually destroy us, acts that develop habits of love, truth, and goodness silently mold and fashion us into the image of God.

When you build a clear, sparkling character, the light reflected through you will pierce the darkness around you.

• •

The integrity of the upright
shall guide them.

PROVERBS 11:3

Adversity causes some men to break;
others to break records.

As a senior in high school, Jim averaged a .427 at bat and led his team in home runs. He also quarterbacked his football team to the state semifinals. Jim later went on to pitch professionally for the New York Yankees.

That's a remarkable achievement for any athlete; but it's an almost unbelievable one for Jim, who was born without a right hand.

A little boy who had only parts of two fingers on one of his hands once came to Jim in the clubhouse after a Yankees' game and said, "They call me 'Crab' at camp. Did kids ever tease you?"

"Yeah," Jim replied. "Kids used to tell me that my hand looked like a foot." Then he asked the boy an all-important question, "Is there anything you can't do?" The boy answered, "No."

"Well, I don't think so either," Jim responded.

Today, what others see as a limitation is only a limitation if *you* think it is. God certainly doesn't see you as limited—He sees you as having unlimited potential. When we begin to see ourselves the way God sees us, there are no records that we can't break!

• •

If thou faint in the day of adversity,

thy strength is small.

PROVERBS 24:10

Learn to say "No"; it will be of more use to you than to be able to read Latin.

The former president of Baylor University, Rufus C. Burleson, once told an audience, "How often I have heard my father paint in glowing words the honesty of his old friend Colonel Ben Sherrod. When he was threatened with bankruptcy and destitution in old age and was staggering under a debt of $850,000, a contemptible lawyer told him, 'Colonel Sherrod, you are hopelessly ruined, but if you will furnish me $5,000 as a witness fee, I can pick a technical flaw in the whole thing and get you out of it.'"

"The grand old Alabamian said, 'Your proposition is insulting. I signed the notes in good faith, and the last dollar shall be paid if charity digs my grave and buys my shroud.' [My father] carried me and my brother Richard once especially to see that incorruptible old man, and his face and words are imprinted upon my heart and brain."

People will remember us for our kept promises and our honesty, especially when we could have profited from not telling the truth. The character of your word is your greatest asset, and honesty is your best virtue.

• •

Just say a simple yes or no
so that you will not sin.

JAMES 5:12 TLB

• •

A man who wants to lead the orchestra
must turn his back on the crowd.

• •

In 1643, a young shoemaker's apprentice
went to Leicestershire, England, for a business
fair. While there, a cousin invited him to share a
jug of beer with him and another friend in the
pub where they had gone to eat. Being thirsty, he
joined them.

After each of the men had drunk a glass
apiece, the man's cousin and friend began to
drink to the health of first this one and then the
other. They agreed that the person who didn't
join in with their toasts would have to pay for the
jug. This shocked the serious shoemaker's apprentice. He rose from the table, took out a coin, and
said simply, "If it be so, I will leave you."

At that, he left the pub and spent much of
the night walking up and down the streets of the
city, praying and crying to the Lord. The Lord

spoke to him these words as recorded in his journal: "Thou seest how young people go together into vanity and old people into the earth. Thou must forsake all—young and old— keep out of all, and be as a stranger unto all." In obedience to this command, the young man left his relations and his home and became a wanderer in England. His name? George Fox, the founder of the Quakers.

If you want to be a leader in life, you will reach a day when you will have to turn your back on people who want to waste their lives. Turn toward those who will lead you, and most of all to the One who will lead you—your Father God.

• •

Come out from among them, and be ye separate, saith the Lord, and touch not the unclean thing; and I will receive you.

2 CORINTHIANS 6:17

> Men are alike in their promises. It is only in their deeds that they differ.

When Teddy Roosevelt was asked to give a speech to the Naval War College in Newport, Rhode Island, on June 2, 1897, his theme was "Readiness." He insisted the only way to keep peace was to be ready for war, and the only way to be ready for war was to enlarge the navy. It was a rousing, patriotic speech. The following February, the Maine was blown up, killing 264 sailors, and Americans across the land cried, "Remember the *Maine!*" In April, President McKinley asked Congress to declare war.

For obvious reasons, Americans were not surprised that Roosevelt backed the war effort. Most Americans *were* surprised, however, when Teddy Roosevelt resigned from his position as assistant secretary of the navy three weeks after the war declaration so that he'd be ready to fight. His friends told him he was crazy for throwing away his political future. His wife was against it. Yet all who knew Roosevelt well knew, even as they made them, that their protests were in vain. He had to join the effort. He later wrote that he wanted to be able to tell his children why he had fought in the war, not why he hadn't fought in it. As far as he was concerned, a person simply couldn't preach one thing and then do another.

That kind of attitude is what will separate you from the pack and cause you to be a great man or woman in life. When your actions line up with your words, a tremendous reputation will follow.

• •

Many a man claims to have unfailing love,
but a faithful man who can find?

PROVERBS 20:6 NIV

Don't cross your bridges until you
get to them. We spend our lives
defeating ourselves crossing
bridges we never get to.

During the four-week siege of Tientsin,
during the Boxer Rebellion of June 1900, Herbert
Hoover helped erect barricades around the
foreign compound and organized all the able-
bodied men into a protective force to man them.
Mrs. Hoover went to work too, helping set up a
hospital, taking her turn nursing the wounded,
rationing food, and serving tea every afternoon
to those on sentry duty. Like her husband, she
remained calm and efficient throughout the
crisis, and even seemed to enjoy the excitement.

One afternoon, while sitting at home playing
solitaire to relax after her work at the hospital, a
shell suddenly burst nearby. She ran to the back
door and discovered a big hole in the backyard. A

little later, a second shell hit the road in front of the house. Then came a third shell. This one burst through one of the windows of the house and demolished a post by the staircase.

Several reporters covering the siege rushed into the living room to see if she was all right and found her calmly seated at the card table. "I don't seem to be winning this hand," she remarked coolly, "but that was the third shell and therefore the last one for the present anyway. Their pattern is three in a row." Then she suggested brightly, "Let's go and have tea."

If you think about it, you will realize most of the things you worry about never happen. Instead of worrying, relax and use your mental energy for more important things.

• •

"Don't be anxious about tomorrow.
God will take care of your tomorrow
too. Live one day at a time."

MATTHEW 6:34 TLB

He that has learned to obey
will know how to command.

The story is told of a great military captain who, after a full day of battle, sat by a warming fire with several of his officers and began talking over the events of the day.

He asked them, "Who did the best today on the field of battle?"

One officer told of a man who had fought bravely all day and then just before dusk had been severely wounded. Another told of a man who had taken a hit for a fellow soldier, sparing his friend's life but possibly losing his own. Yet another told of the man who had led the charge into battle. Still another told of a soldier who had risked his life to pull a fellow soldier into a trench.

The captain heard them out and then said, "No, I fear you are all mistaken. The best man in the field today was the soldier who was just lifting up his arm to strike the enemy, but, upon hearing the trumpet sound the retreat, checked himself, dropped his arm without striking the blow, and retreated. That perfect and ready obedience to the will of his general is the noblest thing that was done today on the battlefield."

That's the kind of obedience God desires from us—immediate and complete.

• •

The wise in heart accept commands,

but a chattering fool comes to ruin.

PROVERBS 10:8 NIV

You must have long-range goals to keep you from being frustrated by short-range failures.

In 1877, George Eastman dreamed that the wonderful world of photography might be accessible to the average person. At the time, photographers working outdoors had to carry multiple pieces of bulky equipment and a corrosive agent called silver nitrate. Eastman theorized that if he could eliminate most of this equipment, he would have something.

Working in a bank by day, he spent his nights reading books on chemistry and magazines about photography. He took foreign language lessons so he could read information published in France and Germany. Then with a partner, he began his own company in 1881. Almost immediately, a problem arose with the new dry plates he had invented. Eastman refunded the money to those who had purchased them and returned to his lab. Three months and 472 experiments later, he came up with the durable emulsion for which he had searched!

Eastman spent many nights sleeping in a hammock at his factory after long days designing equipment. To replace the glass used for photographic plates, he created a roll of thin, flexible material now known as film. To replace heavy tripods, he developed a pocket camera. By 1895, photography was at last available for the common man.

George Eastman's long-term vision kept him motivated even when 471 experiments failed. Keeping your ultimate dream in mind, set short, attainable goals; and before you even know it, your vision will be a reality!

• •

Let us fix our eyes on Jesus, the author and perfecter of our faith, who for the joy set before him endured the cross, scorning its shame, and sat down at the right hand of the throne of God.

HEBREWS 12:2 NIV

··

Clear your mind of can't.

··

Harry Houdini, who won fame as an escape artist early in the twentieth century, issued a challenge wherever he went. He claimed he could be locked in any jail cell in the country and set himself free within minutes. He had done it over and over in every city he visited.

One time, however, something seemed to go wrong. Houdini entered a jail cell in his street clothes. The heavy metal doors clanged shut behind him, and he took from his belt a concealed piece of strong but flexible metal. He set to work on the lock to his cell, but something seemed different about this particular lock. He worked for thirty minutes, but nothing happened. An hour passed. This was long after the time that Houdini normally freed himself, and he began to sweat and pant in exasperation. Still, he could not pick the lock.

Finally, after laboring for two hours, frustrated and feeling a sense of failure closing in around him, Houdini leaned against the door he could not unlock. To his amazement, it swung open! *It had never been locked!*

How many times are challenges impossible—or doors locked—only because we think they are? When we focus our minds and energy toward them and strike the word "can't" from our vocabulary, those impossible tasks turn into attainable goals.

• •

I can do all things through
Christ which strengtheneth me.

PHILIPPIANS 4:13

Grace Hopper was born with a desire to discover how things worked. At age seven, her
curiosity led her to dismantle every clock in her
childhood home! When she grew up, she eventually completed a doctorate in mathematics at Yale
University. During World War II, Grace joined
the navy and was assigned to the navy's computa-
tion project at Harvard University. There she met
"Harvard Mark I," the first fully functional,
digital computing machine. Once again, Grace
set about to learn how something worked.

Unlike the clocks in her childhood home,
however, "Harvard Mark I" had 750 thousand
parts and 500 miles of wire! While most experts
believed computers were too complicated and
expensive for anyone but highly trained scientists
to use, Grace had her own idea. Her goal was to

make them easier to operate so more people could use them. Her work gave rise to the programming language cobol.

As late as 1963, each large computer had its own unique master language. Grace became an advocate for a universally accepted language. She had the audacity to envision a day when computers would one day be small enough to sit on a desk, more powerful than "Harvard Mark I," and useful in offices, schools, and at home. At the age of seventy-nine, she retired from the navy with a rank of rear admiral. More important to her, however, she had lived to see her dream of personal computers come true!

Believe in your dreams. With God, all things are possible.

• •

"Anything is possible if you have faith."

MARK 9:23 TLB

•••••••••••••••••••••••••••••

The future belongs to those
who see possibilities before
they become obvious.

•••••••••••••••••••••••••••••

Eniac was one of the first computers to use
electronic circuits, which made for lightning-fast
calculations. At first, Thomas J. Watson Jr., the
former chairman of IBM, saw no use for it. He
said, "I reacted to Eniac the way some people
probably reacted to the Wright brothers' airplane.
It didn't move me at all. . . . I couldn't see this
gigantic, costly, unreliable device as a piece of
business equipment."

A few weeks later, he and his father wandered
into a research office at IBM and saw an engineer
with a high-speed punch-card machine hooked
up to a black box. When asked what he was
doing, he said, "Multiplying with radio tubes."
The machine was tabulating a payroll at one-
tenth the time it took the standard punch-card
machine to do so. Watson recalls, "That

impressed me as though somebody had hit me on the head with a hammer." He said, "Dad, we should put this thing on the market! Even if we only sell eight or ten, we'll be able to advertise the fact that we have the world's first commercial electronic calculator."

That's how IBM got into electronics. Within a year, they had electronic circuits that both multiplied and divided; and at that point, electronic calculators became truly useful. Thousands of the IBM 604 were sold.

What wasn't yet obvious to Thomas Watson was obvious to the engineer working in the research department. Always keep your eyes and ears open; you never know what you might discover. Look for the possibilities around you.

• •

The vision is yet for an appointed time . . .
it will surely come, it will not tarry.

HABAKKUK 2:3

> When I was a young man I observed that nine out of ten things I did were failures. I didn't want to be a failure, so I did ten times more work.

Early in the 1989 basketball season, Michigan faced Wisconsin. With just seconds left in the fourth quarter, Michigan's Rumeal Robinson found himself at the foul line. His team was trailing by one point, and he knew that if he could sink both shots, Michigan would win. Sadly, Rumeal missed both shots. Wisconsin upset the favored Michigan, and Rumeal went to the locker room feeling devastated and embarrassed.

His dejection, however, spurred him into action and ignited his determination. He decided that at the end of each practice for the rest of the season, he was going to shoot one hundred extra foul shots. Shoot 'em he did!

The moment came when Rumeal stepped to the foul line in yet another game, again with the opportunity to make two shots. This time, there were only three seconds left in overtime, and the game was the NCAA finals! *Swish* went the first shot; and *swish* went the second! Those two points gave Michigan the victory and the Collegiate National Championship for the season.

Have you just failed at something? Don't give up. Instead, work harder. Success is possible!

• •

He becometh poor that dealeth with a slack hand: but the hand of the diligent maketh rich.

PROVERBS 10:4

•••••••••••••••••••••••••••••••

Luck is a matter of preparation
meeting opportunity.

•••••••••••••••••••••••••••••••

We can learn a great deal from the Alaskan
bull moose. Each fall, during the breeding season,
the males of the species battle for dominance.
They literally go head-to-head, antlers crunching
together as they collide. When antlers are broken,
defeat is ensured since a moose's antlers are its
only weapon.

Generally speaking, the heftiest moose with
the largest and strongest antlers wins. Therefore,
the battle is nearly always predetermined the
summer before. It is then that the moose eat
nearly 'round the clock. The one that consumes
the best diet for growing antlers and gaining
weight will be the victor. Those who eat inade-
quately will have weaker antlers and less bulk.
The fight itself involves far more brawn than
brain and more reliance on bulk than on skill.

What is the lesson for us? Spiritual battles are inevitable. We each experience seasons of attack in our lives. Whether we are the victors or the victims depends not on our skills or brainpower but on our spiritual strength. What we do in advance of the war determines the outcome of the battle. Now is the time to develop enduring faith, strength, and wisdom. Now is the time for prayer, reading, and memorizing God's Word. Then, when the opportunity comes, you'll be prepared.

• •

Make the most of every opportunity.

COLOSSIANS 4:5 NIV

• •

Jumping to conclusions is not half as
good an exercise as digging for facts.

• •

Ted Turner is one of the conspicuous personalities of the twentieth century. He turned
Channel 17 in Atlanta into the first "Super
Station," transmitting its signal to cable systems
nationwide via satellite. Soon after, he purchased
the Atlanta Braves baseball team and the Atlanta
Hawks basketball team. In 1980, he originated
CNN, the world's first live, 'round-the-clock, all-
news television network. He organized the
Inaugural Goodwill Olympic Games in Moscow,
has won numerous awards, and has held national
and world sailing titles.

About making choices and decisions, Ted has
given this advice, "There is a saying, 'Be sure of
your information, then go ahead.' My father was
the first one who pointed this out to me. . . . Get
all the information you can, along with the

advice and counsel of people you think are wise. This is a prerequisite for success in the long haul. You should not make decisions until you have complete knowledge about things. [When] you have to form opinions without as much information as you should have, or without firsthand knowledge . . . don't hold hard and fast opinions. When new information becomes available, you should be able to change your mind."

That is wise advice. Jumped-to conclusions are usually based on speculation—not truth. The person who comes out on top is going to be the one who not only knows all the facts but most importantly, knows the truth.

• •

Study to shew thyself approved unto God, a workman that needeth not to be ashamed, rightly dividing the word of truth.

2 TIMOTHY 2:15

The most valuable of all
talents is that of never using
two words when one will do.

Albert Einstein is reputed to have had a
wholesome disregard for the tyranny of custom.
One evening, the president of Swarthmore
College hosted a dinner held in Einstein's honor.
Although he was not scheduled to speak during
the event—only to receive an award—after the
award was made, the audience clamored,
"Speech, speech!" The president turned the
podium over to him. Einstein reluctantly came
forward and said only this: "Ladies and gentlemen, I am very sorry but I have nothing to say."
And then he sat down.

A few seconds later, he stood back up and
said, "In case I do have something to say, I'll
come back."

Some six months later, Einstein wired the president of the college with this message: "Now I have something to say."

Another dinner was held, and this time, Einstein made a speech.

If you have nothing to say, it's wise to say nothing. If you do have something to say, it's wise to say it in as few words as possible. As the old saying goes, "If your mind should go blank, don't forget to turn off the sound."

• •

In the multitude of words there wanteth not sin: but he that refraineth his lips is wise.

PROVERBS 10:19

• 117 •

Laziness is often mistaken for patience.

Henry Ward Beecher, one of the most powerful preachers in American history, gave this illustration in one of his sermons:

"The lobster, when left high and dry among the rocks, has no sense and energy enough to work his way back to the sea, but waits for the sea to come to him. If it does not come, he remains where he is, and dies, although the slightest exertion would enable him to reach the waves, which are perhaps tossing and tumbling within a yard of him.

"There is a tide in human affairs that casts men into 'tight places,' and leaves them there, like stranded lobsters. If they choose to lie where the breakers have flung them, expecting some grand billow to take them on its big shoulders and carry them to smooth water, the chances are that their hopes will never be realized."

Laziness is doing nothing, hoping nothing, being nothing. Patience, on the other hand, doesn't mean not doing anything. It means working on in hope that what you're waiting for will eventually come to pass, but you will continue to work on even if it doesn't.

• •

Let us lay aside every weight, and the sin which doth so easily beset us, and let us run with patience the race that is set before us.

HEBREWS 12:1

. . . .

One-half the trouble of this life can
be traced to saying "yes" too quick,
and not saying "no" soon enough.

. . . .

A man who had been quite successful in the
manufacturing business decided to retire. He
called in his son to tell him of his decision,
saying, "Son, it's all yours as of the first of next
month." The son, while eager to take over the
firm and exert his own brand of leadership, also
realized what a big responsibility he was facing.
"I'd be grateful for any words of advice you have
to give me," he said to his father.

The father advised, "Well, I've made a success
of this business because of two principles: reliability and wisdom. First, take reliability. If you
promise goods by the tenth of the month, no
matter what happens, you must deliver by the
tenth. Your customers won't understand any
delay. They'll see a delay as failure. So even if it

costs you overtime, double time, or golden time, you must deliver on your promise."

The son mulled this over for a few moments and then asked, "And wisdom?" The father shot back: "Wisdom is never making such a stupid promise in the first place."

Carefully weigh your ability to back up your words with evidence, and be sure you can deliver on a promise before you make it. A large part of your reputation is your ability to keep your word.

• •

Seest thou a man that is hasty in his words?
there is more hope of a fool than of him.

PROVERBS 29:20

I would rather fail in the cause that
someday will triumph than triumph
in a cause that someday will fail

When Honorious was emperor of Rome, the
great Coliseum was often filled to overflowing
with spectators who came from near and far to
watch the state-sponsored games. Part of the
sport consisted of human beings doing battle
with wild beasts or one another—to the death.
The assembled multitudes made holiday of such
sport and found the greatest delight when a
human being died.

One such day, a Syrian monk named
Telemachus was part of the vast crowd in the
arena. Telemachus was cut to the core by the
utter disregard he saw for the value of human
life. He leaped from the spectator stands into the
arena during a gladiatorial show and cried out,
"This thing is not right! This thing must stop!"

Because he had interfered, the authorities commanded that Telemachus be run through with a sword, which was done. He died but not in vain. His cry kindled a small flame in the nearly burned-out conscience of the people, and within a matter of months, the gladiatorial combats came to an end.

The greater the wrong, the louder we must cry out against it. The finer the cause, the louder we must applaud.

● ●

Thanks be unto God, which always causeth us to triumph in Christ.

2 CORINTHIANS 2:14

Carve your name on hearts and not on marble.

When Salvation Army officer Shaw saw the three men before him, tears sprang to his eyes. Shaw was a medical missionary who had just arrived in India. He had been assigned to a leper colony that the Salvation Army was taking over. The three men before him had manacles and fetters binding their hands and feet. Their bonds were painfully cutting into their diseased flesh. Captain Shaw turned to the guard and said, "Please unfasten the chains."

"It isn't safe," the guard protested. "These men are dangerous criminals as well as lepers!"

"I'll be responsible," Captain Shaw said. "They are suffering enough." He then reached out, took the keys, knelt, tenderly removed the shackles from the men, and treated their bleeding ankles and wrists.

About two weeks later, Shaw had to make an overnight trip. He dreaded leaving his wife and child alone. The words of the guard came back to him, and he was concerned about the safety of his family. When Shaw's wife went to the front door the morning she was alone, she was startled to see the three criminals lying on her steps. One of them explained, "We know the doctor go. We stay here all night so no harm come to you."

Even dangerous men are capable of responding to an act of love! Touched lives are the most important monuments you can leave. When you treat people with that kind of love, you are impressing your name upon their hearts.

• •

The only letter I need is you yourselves!
... They can see that you are a letter
from Christ, written by us ... not one
carved on stone, but in human hearts.

2 CORINTHIANS 3:2–3 TLB

A knowledge of the Bible without a college course is more valuable than a college course without the Bible.

A Bible—carefully read and well worn—was the most important book in Gerrit's house. His home was a house of prayer, where many tears were shed in intercession for revival in his church in Heemstede. Almost a generation later, his prayers were answered as that very church became the center of an upsurge of faith in Holland— part of the Great Awakening in Europe.

When she was about eighteen years old, Gerrit's great-granddaughter had a dream about him. He was walking through a beautiful park with her, and he said, "When you sow some seed and put it in the ground, this seed will make a plant, and this plant will give seed again. . . . You, my dear Corrie, are the daughter of my grand-son. . . . You are a plant, blooming from my seed.

I will show you something that will never be changed. It is the Word of God." In the dream, he opened his Bible and said, "This book will be the same forever." He then told her, "Plant the seeds from God's Book, and they will grow from generation to generation."

Corrie ten Boom did just that. She planted God's Word in hearts and minds around the world. Information learned in textbooks is continually updated, and courses of study change; but the truths of the Bible are absolutes. Its promises are sure. Plant its seeds in your heart.

• •

All scripture is given by inspiration of God,
and is profitable for doctrine, for reproof,
for correction, for instruction in righteousness:
That the man of God may be perfect, thoroughly
furnished unto all good works.

2 TIMOTHY 3:16–17

> Little minds are tamed and
> subdued by misfortune; but
> great minds rise above them.

When Aaron was eight months old, he stopped gaining weight. A few months later, his hair began to fall out. At first, doctors told Aaron's parents that he would be short as an adult but otherwise normal. Later, a pediatrician diagnosed the problem as progeria, or rapid aging. Just as the pediatrician predicted, Aaron never grew beyond three feet in height, had no hair on his head or body, looked like an old man while still a child, and died of old age in his early teens. His father, a rabbi, felt a deep, aching sense of unfairness.

About a year and a half after Aaron's death, the father came to realize that none of us is ever promised a life free of pain or disappointment. Rather, the most any of us has been promised is that we need not be alone in our pain and that we can draw upon a source outside ourselves for strength and courage. He came to the conclusion that God does not cause our misfortunes but rather helps us by inspiring others to help.

Out of Harold Kushner's experience came a book that has helped millions, *When Bad Things Happen to Good People.* He says, "I think of Aaron and all that his life taught me, and I realize how much I have lost and how much I have gained. Yesterday seems less painful, and I am not afraid of tomorrow."

When you stop looking at the difficulties in your life as obstacles and start seeing them as stepping stones, you will begin to rise above your difficulties and gain something from them. They will make you stronger and wiser.

• •

A just man falleth seven times,

and riseth up again.

PROVERBS 24:16

There is no poverty that
can overtake diligence.

• •

A young reporter once interviewed a successful businessman. The reporter asked the man
to give him a detailed history of his company. As
the man talked at length, the reporter began to
be amazed at the enormity of the many problems
the man had overcome. He finally asked him,
"But how did you overcome so many problems of
such great magnitude?"

The old gentleman leaned back in his chair
and said, "There's really no trick to it." Then he
added, "You know . . . there are some troubles
that seem so high you can't climb over them."
The reporter nodded in agreement, thinking of
several he was currently facing. "And," the wise
businessman went on, "there are some troubles
so wide you can't walk around them." Again, the
reporter nodded. The man went on, raising his

voice dramatically, "And there are some problems so deep you can't dig under them." Eager for a solution, the reporter said, "Yes? Yes?"

"It's then," the man concluded, "that you know the only way to beat the problem is to duck your head and wade right through it."

A problem rarely decreases in size while a person stands and stares at it; but when you diligently pursue a solution, your problem is guaranteed to shrink.

• •

He becometh poor that dealeth
with a slack hand: but the hand
of the diligent maketh rich.

PROVERBS 10:4

American sports fans watched in awe on Sunday, March 4, 1979, as Phil took to the giant-slalom slopes at Whiteface Mountain, New York. He exploded onto the course and then settled into a powerful carving of the mountainside. Nonetheless, at gate thirty-five, tragedy struck. Phil hooked his inside ski on a pole, went flying head over heels, and crashed in a crumpled heap. The ski team physician described the injury as "the ultimate broken ankle"—a break of both the ankle and lower leg. He had to put the bones back together with a three-inch metal plate and seven screws.

The question was not whether Phil would ever ski again but if he would ever walk again. Looking back, Phil describes the months after his injury as a time of deep despair. Still, he never entertained doubts about walking or skiing.

After two months on crutches and a high-discipline exercise program, he forced himself to walk without limping. In August, he began skiing gentle slopes. Less than six months after the accident, he entered a race in Australia and finished second. In February of 1980, less than a year after his agonizing injury, Phil Mahre took on the same mountain where he had fallen, and he won an Olympic silver medal.

When defeat and despair threaten to overtake you and squash your dreams, keep on going. Eventually, you will overtake defeat with victory and despair with joy!

• •

As for you, be strong and do not give up,
for your work will be rewarded.

2 Chronicles 15:7 niv

> You can accomplish more in one hour
> with God than one lifetime without Him.

The Lord appeared to a man named Ananias in a vision and asked him to undertake what Ananias must surely have perceived as a dangerous mission. He directed him to go to the house of a man named Judas, lay his hands on a man named Saul of Tarsus, and pray that he might receive his sight. Saul had been blinded while traveling to Damascus to persecute the Christians there, having the full intent of taking them captive to Jerusalem for trial, torture, and death. Even so, Ananias did as the Lord asked him, and within the hour, Saul's sight was restored.

According to Christian legend, Ananias was a simple cobbler who had no idea what happened to Saul after that day, or how he had changed the course of human history by obeying God in a simple act that was part of Saul's transformation into the apostle Paul. As he lay on his deathbed, Ananias looked up toward Heaven and whispered, "I haven't done much, Lord: a few shoes sewn, a few sandals stitched. But what more could be expected of a poor cobbler?"

The Lord spoke in Ananias' heart, "Don't worry, Ananias, about how much you have accomplished—or how little. You were there in the hour I needed you, and that is all that matters."

Being in the right place at the right time, even if it's only for one hour, can give you the opportunity to change history. In order to be there, you must simply listen and obey.

• •

With God all things are possible.

MATTHEW 19:26

If you don't stand for something, you'll fall for anything!

Former President Harry S Truman once remarked that no president of our nation has ever escaped abuse and even libel from the press. He noted that is was far more common than rare to find a president publicly called a traitor. Truman further concluded that the president who had not fought with Congress or the Supreme Court hadn't done his job.

What is true for an American president is also true for everyone else. No matter how small a person's job may be—no matter how low he may be on a particular organizational chart or strata of society—there will be those who oppose him, ridicule him, and perhaps even challenge him to a fight. That is why no person can expect to conduct himself as if he were trying to win a popularity contest. Rather, a person needs to chart the course he feels compelled to walk in life and then do so with head held high and his convictions intact. It's simply a matter of taking life in stride to recognize that every person will eventually face the test of ridicule and criticism as he upholds his principles or defends his morals.

It's inevitable that you will be criticized or attacked sometime in your life, but collapsing from *fear* of an attack isn't inevitable. Stand firm in your faith, and the Lord will stand with you!

• •

If you do not stand firm in your faith,
you will not stand at all.

ISAIAH 7:9 NIV

The difference between ordinary and extraordinary is that little extra.

Country-music star Randy Travis and his manager, Lib, remember the lean days of his career—all 3,650 of them. For ten years, Lib did whatever it took to keep her club open long enough for somebody to discover Travis' talent. For his part, Randy sang his heart out, and when he wasn't singing, he fried catfish or washed dishes in the kitchen. Then it happened. Everything seemed to click for him. He had a hit called "On the Other Hand," an album contract, a tour offer, and a movie deal. He was hot! Everyone seemed to be calling him an overnight success.

Travis notes, "We were turned down more than once by every label in Nashville, but I'm kind of one to believe that if you work at something long enough and keep believing, sooner or later it will happen."

In many instances in life, it's extra effort that makes the difference. Money can buy a house, but loving touches turn it into a home. A sack lunch can be a gourmet meal with a love note tucked inside. A meal is just food, but with candles and flowers, it's an occasion. Do more than is required of you today. Give the extra that makes life truly extraordinary.

• •

Whatsoever thy hand findeth to do,

do it with thy might.

ECCLESIASTES 9:10

Man cannot discover new oceans
unless he has the courage
to lose sight of the shore.

Two baseball coaches were commiserating
about the difficulty of recruiting quality players
for their teams. Said one coach, "If only I could
find a man who plays every position perfectly,
always gets a hit, never strikes out, and never
makes a fielding error." The other coach sighed in
agreement and added, "Yeah, if we could just get
him to lay down his hot dog and come down out
of the stands."

Playing life's game to the fullest requires taking
risks. Without risk, life has little emotion, little that
can be counted as exhilarating or fulfilling.

- To laugh is to risk appearing the fool.
- To weep is to risk appearing sentimental.
- To reach out for another is to risk
  involvement.

- To expose feelings is to risk exposing one's true self.
- To place ideas and dreams before a crowd is to risk ridicule.
- To love is to risk not being loved in return.
- To live is to risk dying.
- To hope is to risk despair.
- To try is to risk failure.

Yet the person who risks nothing does nothing, has nothing, and ultimately becomes nothing. Don't be afraid to go for it. Get down out of the stands and play ball!

Peter got out of the boat, and walked on the water and came toward Jesus.

MATTHEW 14:29 NASB

Fads come and go; wisdom
and character go on forever.

Many years ago in South Africa, a man sold his farm so that he might spend his days in search of diamonds. He was consumed with dreams of becoming wealthy. When he had finally exhausted his resources and his health and was no closer to his fortune than the day he sold his farm, he threw himself into a river and drowned.

One day, the man who had bought his farm spotted an unusual-looking stone in a creek bed. He placed it on his fireplace mantle as a conversation piece. A visitor noticed the stone and examined it closely. He then voiced his suspicion that the stone was actually a diamond. The discreet farmer had the stone analyzed, and sure enough, it was one of the largest and finest diamonds ever found.

Still operating with great secrecy, the farmer searched his stream, gathering similar stones. They were all diamonds. In fact, his farm was covered with diamonds just waiting to be picked up! The farm the diamond seeker had sold turned out to be one of the richest diamond deposits in the world.

The lessons of wisdom can often be learned in the relationships and experiences we encounter every day. Ask God to reveal to you what you need to know in order to live the life He desires. The resources you need are probably right in front of you.

• •

O my son, be wise and stay in God's paths.

PROVERBS 23:19 TLB

Perseverance is a great element
of success; if you only knock long
enough and loud enough at the gate,
you are sure to wake up somebody.

We all know the power of gravity. When we
drop a hammer, it hits our toes; it never floats
upward. We fall down not up. What many of us
don't realize is that the gravitational *energy* of the
whole earth has been estimated to amount to
only a millionth of a horsepower! A toy magnet
in the hands of a child probably has thousands of
times more energy.

What gravity lacks in energy, however, it makes
up in tenacity. Gravity simply refuses to let go.

Not only is gravity tenacious, but it has far-
reaching effects. Gravitational pull appears to be
virtually limitless, reaching across the universe
with nearly unimaginable power. Gravitational

pull is what keeps the moon orbiting the earth, the planets revolving around the sun, and the sun—along with a billion other stars—rotating around the center of our galaxy like a cosmic pinwheel.

You may not have a great deal of power or energy today, but as the popular phrase states, you can "hang in there."

Don't stop believing! Don't give up hope! Eventually the door will be opened.

● ●

Ask, and it shall be given you;

seek, and ye shall find; knock,

and it shall be opened unto you.

LUKE 11:9

In March of 1987, Eamon Coughlan was running in a qualifying heat at the World Indoor Track Championships in Indianapolis. The Irishman was the reigning world-record holder at fifteen hundred meters, and he was favored to win the race handily. Unfortunately, with two-and-a-half laps left to run, he was tripped and fell hard. Even so, he got up and with great effort, he managed to catch the race leaders. With only twenty yards to go, he was in third place, which would have been good enough to qualify for the final race.

Then Coughlan looked over his shoulder to the inside. Seeing no one there, he relaxed his effort slightly. What he hadn't noticed, however, was that a runner was charging hard on the outside. This runner passed Coughlan just a yard before the finish line, thus eliminating him from the finals.

Coughlan's great comeback effort ended up being worthless for one and only one reason: he momentarily took his eyes off the finish line and focused on the would-be competitors instead.

One of the most important factors in reaching your goals in life is to have single-minded focus. Don't let yourself become distracted by what others do or say. Run your race to win!

• •

I have fought a good fight, I have finished my course, I have kept the faith.

2 TIMOTHY 4:7

It needs more skill than I can tell to play the second fiddle well

People often think of heart surgeons as being the arrogant prima donnas of the medical world. Those who know Dr. William DeVries, the surgeon who pioneered the artificial heart, couldn't *disagree* more. Coworkers at Humana Hospital Audubon in Louisville, Kentucky, describe DeVries as the kind of doctor who shows up on Sundays just to cheer up discouraged patients. He occasionally changes dressings, traditionally considered a nurse's job; and if a patient wants him to stick around and talk, he always does.

Friends say DeVries is an old shoe who fits in wherever he goes. He likes to wear cowboy boots with his surgical scrubs, and he often repairs hearts to the beat of Vivaldi or jazz. "He has always got a smile lurking," says Louisville cardiologist Dr. Robert Goodin, "and he's always looking for a way to let it out."

No matter how high you rise, never forget that you started out at ground zero. Even if you were born to great wealth and privilege, you still were born as a helpless babe. Real success comes not in thinking you have arrived at a place where others should serve you, but in recognizing that in whatever place you are, you have arrived at a position where you can serve others.

* *

He that is greatest among
you shall be your servant.

MATTHEW 23:11

> A man never discloses his
> own character so clearly as
> when he describes another's.

After several months of romance, Napoleon and Josephine decided to marry. The notary who made out the marriage contract was one of Josephine's friends. He secretly advised her against marrying "an obscure little officer who has nothing besides his uniform and sword and has no future." He thought she should find someone of greater worth. With her charms, he advised, she might attract a wealthy man, perhaps an army contractor or a business investor.

Napoleon was in the next room while the notary was giving this advice to his beloved. He could hear every word that said. Still, he did not disclose he had overheard. Years later, however, he had his revenge.

After his coronation as Emperor, this same notary appeared before him on a matter of business. At the conclusion of their appointment, Napoleon smiled and observed that Madame de Beauharnais—now that she was queen of France—had done very well, after all, to have married that "obscure little officer who possessed nothing besides his uniform and sword and had no future."

The notary was forced to agree that Madame, indeed, had done well. As for himself, he was still a notary!

Be careful before you pass judgment on another. You're revealing something about yourself, and your words may come back to bite you.

● ●

A good man out of the good treasure of
the heart bringeth forth good things:
and an evil man out of the evil treasure
bringeth forth evil things.

MATTHEW 12:35

> The greatest use of life is
> to spend it for something
> that will outlast it.

Although we do not have the original man-
uscripts of the New Testament, we do have more
than 99.9 percent of the original text because of
the faithful work of manuscript copyists over
the centuries.

Copying was a long, arduous process. In
ancient days, copyists did not sit at desks while
writing, but rather stood or made copies while
sitting on benches or stools, holding a scroll on
their knees. Notes at the end of some scrolls tell
of the drudgery of the work:

- "He who does not know how to write sup-
  poses it to be no labor; but though only
  three fingers write, the whole body labors."
- "Writing bows one's back, thrusts the ribs into
  one's stomach, and fosters a general debility."

- "As travelers rejoice to see their home country, so also is the end of a book to those who toil."

Even so, without the work of faithful copyists, we would not have the Christian Scriptures today. As one scribe aptly noted: "There is no scribe who will not pass away, but what his hands have written will remain forever."

If you truly want your work to last, do work that touches the eternal truth and nature of God.

• •

"Store up for yourselves treasures in heaven, where moth and rust do not destroy, and where thieves do not break in and steal."

MATTHEW 6:20 NIV

> Every man's work, whether it be
> literature, or music, or pictures,
> or architecture, or anything else,
> is always a portrait of himself.

A young man once made an appointment with a well-published author. The first question the author asked him was, "Why did you want to see me?"

The young man stammered, "Well, I'm a writer too. I was hoping you could share with me some of your secrets for successful writing."

The author asked a second question, "What have you written?"

"Nothing," the young man replied, "at least nothing that is finished yet."

The author asked a third question, "Well, if you haven't written, then tell me, what are you writing?"

The young man replied, "Well, I'm in school right now, so I'm not writing anything at present."

The author then asked a fourth question, "So why do you call yourself a writer?"

Writers write. Composers compose. Painters paint. Workmen work. What you do to a great extent defines who you are and what you become. What does your work say about you? When your work on the outside coincides with who you are on the inside, you have found your true purpose in life and will find ultimate fulfillment.

• •

As in water face reflects face,

So the heart of man reflects man.

PROVERBS 27:19 NASB

> What we do on some great occasion will probably depend on what we already are; and what we are will be the result of precious years of self-discipline.

During a homecoming football game against rival Concordia, Augsburg College found itself losing miserably. Late in the fourth quarter, however, nose guard David Stevens came off the bench and sparked a fire. He initiated or assisted in two tackles, and when a Concordia player fumbled the ball, David fell on it. As he held the recovered ball high, the crowd roared. It was an unforgettable moment for Augsburg fans!

David Lee Stevens was born to a woman who had taken thalidomide, an anti-nausea drug given to many pregnant women in the early 60s that was quickly proven to cause severe birth defects. David's feet appeared where his legs should have started. Abandoned by his mother, David was adopted by a foster family. Bee and Bill Stevens imposed strict rules of behavior on David, nurtured him, and loved him. They insisted he learn to do things for himself, and they never put him in a wheelchair. At age three, he was fitted with "legs."

In school, David became a student leader, made good grades, organized special events, and befriended new students. In high school, he not only played football but baseball, basketball, and hockey. He became a champion wrestler. When offered handicap license plates, he refused them, stating simply, "Those are for people who need them. I am not 'disabled.'"

David was taught to discipline himself, and so he was able to perform, in spite of his apparent handicap. Whatever obstacle may be in your way, self-discipline can help you either rise above it or plow right through it.

• •

I keep under my body, and
bring it into subjection.

1 CORINTHIANS 9:27

> Our deeds determine us, as much
> as we determine our deeds.

In the fourth round of a national spelling bee in Washington, eleven-year-old Rosalie Elliot, a champion from South Carolina, was asked to spell the word *avowal*. Her soft Southern accent made it difficult for the judges to determine if she had used an *a* or an *e* as the next-to-last letter of the word. They deliberated for several minutes and also listened to tape-recorded playbacks, but they still couldn't determine which letter had been pronounced. Finally the chief judge, John Lloyd, put the question to the only person who knew the answer. He asked Rosalie, "Was the letter an *a* or an *e*?"

Rosalie, surrounded by whispering young spellers, knew by now the correct spelling of the word; but without hesitation, she replied that she had misspelled the word and had used an *e*.

As she walked from the stage, the entire audience stood and applauded her honesty and integrity, including dozens of newspaper reporters covering the event. While Rosalie had not won the contest, she had definitely come out a winner that day.

We often think that who we are determines what we do. Equally true, what you do today will determine, in part, who you become tomorrow.

• •

Even a child is known by his actions,
by whether his conduct is pure and right.
PROVERBS 20:11 NIV

• •

What you do speaks so loud that
I cannot hear what you say.

• •

During the Korean War, a South Korean
civilian was arrested by the communists and sentenced to execution. When the young communist
leader learned that the prisoner in his charge
was the head of an orphanage caring for young
children, he decided to spare him, but ordered
that the man's son be executed in his place. The
nineteen-year-old boy was shot in the presence
of his father.

After the war, the United Nations captured
the young communist leader. He was tried for his
war crimes and condemned to death. Before the
sentence could be carried out, however, the
Christian whose son had been killed pleaded for
the life of the killer. He argued that the communist had been young when he ordered the execution and that he really didn't know what he was

doing. "Give him to me," the man requested, "and I will train him."

The United Nations forces granted the unusual request, and the father took the murderer of his son into his own home and cared for him. The young communist eventually became a Christian pastor.

For good or for bad, what we do speaks loudly. How vital it is that we do what we say!

• •

Show me your faith without deeds, and
I will show you my faith by what I do.

JAMES 2:18 NIV

•••••••••••••••••••••••••••

All virtue is summed up in dealing justly.

•••••••••••••••••••••••••••

To crack the lily white system of higher education in Georgia in the 1960s, black leaders decided they needed to find only two squeaky-clean students who couldn't be challenged on moral, intellectual, or educational grounds. In a discussion about who might be chosen, Alfred Holmes immediately volunteered his son, Hamilton, the top black male senior in the city. Charlayne Hunter-Gault also stepped forward and expressed an interest in applying to the university. Georgia delayed admitting both boys on grounds it had no room in its dormitories, and the matter eventually ended up in federal court. Judge Bootle ordered the university to admit the two, who were qualified in every respect; and thus, segregation ended at the university level in that state and soon the nation.

Attorney General Robert Kennedy declared in a speech not long after: "We know that it is the law which enables men to live together, that creates order out of chaos. . . . And we know that if one man's rights are denied, the rights of all are endangered."

Justice may be universal, but it always begins at the individual level. Is there someone that you might treat more justly today?

• •

He hath shewed thee, O man, what is good;
and what doth the LORD require of thee,
but to do justly, and to love mercy,
and to walk humbly with thy God?

MICAH 6:8

No matter what a man's past may
have been, his future is spotless.

Willingway Hospital is one of the nation's
top treatment centers for alcoholism and drug
addiction. There would be no Willingway,
however, if it weren't for Dot and John, who at
one time seemed the least likely candidates to
found such a hospital. Early in their courtship,
Dot and John drank heavily, and after they
married, they began taking amphetamines. John,
a medical doctor, was arrested for writing himself
narcotics prescriptions. He spent six months in
prison, eventually falling on his knees and crying
out to God for help in overcoming his addictions.

When John returned to medical practice drug
free and alcohol free, he began to receive referrals
from other doctors to treat their alcoholic
patients. Dot and John set up three beds under
the chandelier in their own dining room as a

detox room. Among their patients have been three of their own four children, each of whom struggled with addictions.

As word of their compassion spread, they established a forty-bed hospital on eleven acres close to their home. The chandelier still hangs in the detox room as a symbol of hope. All four children have worked on the medical staff or administration of Willingway. With God's help, they truly became a family in full recovery.

Regardless of our past, the future is a blank slate, waiting to be written upon.

● ●

Forgetting those things which are behind, and reaching forth unto those things which are before.

PHILIPPIANS 3:13

• •

One of Life's great rules is this:
The more you give, the more you get.

• •

Three young men were each given three
kernels of corn by a wise old sage, who admon-
ished them to go out into the world and use the
corn to bring themselves good fortune.

The first young man put his three kernels of
corn into a bowl of hot broth and ate them. The
second thought, *I can do better than that,* and he
planted his three kernels of corn. Within a few
months, he had three stalks of corn. He took the
ears of corn from the stalks, boiled them, and
had enough corn for three meals.

The third man said to himself, *I can do better
than that!* He also planted his three kernels of
corn; but when his three stalks of corn produced,
he stripped one of the ears and replanted all of
the seeds in it, gave the second ear of corn to a
sweet maiden, and ate the third. His one full ear's

worth of replanted corn kernels gave him 200 stalks of corn! The kernels of these he continued to replant, setting aside only a bare minimum to eat. He eventually planted a hundred acres of corn. With his fortune, he not only won the hand of the sweet maiden but also purchased the land owned by the sweet maiden's father. He never hungered again.

If you want to receive in life, you must first learn to give.

• •

The liberal soul shall be made fat: and he that watereth shall be watered also himself.

PROVERBS 11:25

> Everything comes to him
> who hustles while he waits.

In 1928, a happy, ambitious young nursing student was diagnosed with tuberculosis. Her family sent her to a nursing home in Saranac Lake for several months of curing. She would remain in bed for twenty-one years! Most people may have given up, but not Isabel Smith. She approached the threshold of death on several occasions, but she never ceased to pursue the art of living. She read voraciously, loved to write letters, studied geography, and taught other patients to read and write. From her bed, she studied atomic energy with a fellow patient, a young physicist, and organized a town hall meeting on the topic.

While ill, she met a kind, gentle man, who was also a patient at the sanitarium. She dreamed of marrying him and having a little house "under the mountains." At her lowest ebb, her dream kept her going, and in 1948, they did marry. She then wrote a book about "all the good things life has brought me." *Wish I Might,* published in 1955, earned her enough in royalties to buy her mountain retreat.

A tragic life? Hardly! Isabel Smith achieved everything she set out to achieve, even when the odds against her were a thousand to one. Even flat on her back in bed, she never quit growing, learning, and giving.

• •

We do not want you to become lazy, but to imitate those who through faith and patience inherit what has been promised.

HEBREWS 6:12 NIV

> A well-trained memory is one that permits you to forget everything that isn't worth remembering.

According to an old legend, two monks named Tanzan and Ekido were traveling together down a muddy road one day. Heavy monsoon rains had saturated the area, and they were grateful for a few moments of sunshine to make their journey. Before long, they came around a bend and encountered a lovely girl in a silk kimono. She looked extremely forlorn as she stared at the muddy road before her.

At once, Tanzan responded to her plight. "Come here, girl," he said. Then lifting her in his arms, he carried her over the slippery ooze and set her down on the other side of the road.

Ekido didn't speak again to Tanzan. It was apparent to Tanzan that something was bothering him deeply, but try as he would, he couldn't get

Ekido to talk to him. Then that night after they reached their intended lodging, Ekido could no longer restrain his anger and disappointment. "We monks don't go near females," he said to Tanzan in an accusing voice. "We especially don't go near young and lovely maidens. It is dangerous. Why did you do that?"

"I left the girl back there, Ekido," replied Tanzan. Then he asked the key question, "Are you still carrying her?"

Train your mind to think on pure things. Make a conscious decision to stop any thought that doesn't line up with the teachings of the Bible. Take those thoughts captive! (See 2 Corinthians 10:5.)

• •

Finally, brethren, whatsoever things are true, whatsoever things are honest, whatsoever things are just . . . if there be any virtue, and if there be any praise, think on these things.

PHILIPPIANS 4:8

Defeat is not the worst of failures.
.Not to have tried is the true failure.

There once was a young man who lived a most miserable life. Orphaned before he was three, he was taken in by strangers. He was kicked out of school, suffered from poverty, and as the result of inherited physical weaknesses, he developed serious heart trouble as a teenager. His beloved wife died early in their marriage. He lived as an invalid most of his adult life, and he eventually died at the young age of forty. By all outward appearances, he was defeated by life and doomed to be forgotten by history.

Even so, he never quit trying to express himself and to achieve success over the twenty years of his active work life. In that period, he produced some of the most brilliant articles, essays, and criticisms ever written. His poetry is still read widely and studied by virtually every

high school student in the United States. His
short stories and detective stories are famous.
One of his poems, on display at the famous
Huntington Library in California, has been
valued at more than fifty thousand dollars, which
is far more than the young man earned in his
entire lifetime.

His name? Edgar Allan Poe.

Circumstances don't affect your chances for
success nearly as much as your level of effort!

• •

Be strong and of a good courage; be not afraid,
neither be thou dismayed: for the LORD thy
God is with thee withersoever thou goest.

JOSHUA 1:9

> Unless you try to do something
> beyond what you have already
> mastered, you will never grow.

After falling twice in the 1988 Olympic speed-skating races, Dan Jansen sought out sports psychologist Dr. Jim Loehr, who helped him find a new balance between sport and life, and who helped him pay more attention to the mental aspects of skating. Peter Mueller became his coach, putting him through workouts that Dan has since described as the "toughest I've ever known." By the time the 1994 Olympics arrived, Jansen had more confidence than ever. He had set a five-hundred-meter world record just two months before. That race seemed to be all his!

During the five-hundred-meter race, Jansen fell. He was shaken. Dr. Loehr immediately advised, "Start preparing for the one thousand. Put the five hundred behind you immediately.

Stop reliving it." The one thousand! For years Dan had felt he could not win at that distance. He had always considered it his weaker event. Now it was his last chance for an Olympic medal. "As the race began," Jansen said, "I just seemed to be sailing along," and then he slipped and came within an inch of stepping on a lane marker. Still, he didn't panic. He raced on and recorded a world-record time that won him the gold medal!

Once you reach a goal or master a skill, set your sights higher. As you approach each goal, set a new one. Don't be intimidated! Your toughest goal can become your greatest triumph.

• •

Reaching forth unto those things which are before, I press toward the mark for the prize of the high calling of God in Christ Jesus.

PHILIPPIANS 3:13–14

I don't know the secret to success,
but the key to failure is
to try to please everyone.

A young man once studied violin under a
world-renowned violinist and master teacher. He
worked hard for several years at perfecting his
talent, and the day finally came when he was
called upon to give his first major public recital
in the large city where both he and his teacher
lived. Following each selection, which he performed with great skill and passion, the per-
former seemed uneasy about the great applause
he received. Even though he knew that those in
the audience were musically astute and not likely
to give such applause to a less than superior performance, the young man acted almost as if he
couldn't hear the appreciation that was being
showered upon him.

At the close of the last number, the applause was thunderous and numerous "Bravos" were shouted, but the talented young violinist had his eyes glued on one spot only. Finally, when an elderly man in the first row of the balcony smiled and nodded to him in approval, the young man relaxed and beamed with both relief and joy. His teacher had praised his work! The applause of thousands meant nothing until he had first won the approval of the master.

Who are you trying to please today? You will never be able to please everyone, but you can please the One who matters most—your Father God. Keep your eyes on Him, and you can't fail.

• •

Am I now trying to win the
approval of men, or of God?

GALATIANS 1:10 NIV

Kites rise highest against the wind, not with it.

The engineers hired to build a suspension bridge across the Niagara River faced a serious problem: how to get the first cable from one side of the river to the next. The river was too wide to throw a cable across it and too swift to cross by boat.

An engineer finally came up with a solution! With a favoring stiff wind, a kite was lofted and allowed to drift over the river and land on the opposite shore. Attached to the kite was a very light string, which was threaded through the kite's tip so that both ends of the string were in the hands of the kite flyer. Once the kite was in the hand of engineers on the far side, they removed the kite from its string and set up a pulley. A small rope was attached to one end of the original kite string and pulled across the river. At the end of this string, a piece of rope was attached and pulled across and so on until a cable strong enough to sustain the iron cable, which supported the bridge, could be drawn across the water.

Let your faith soar like that kite! Release it to God, believing that He can and will help you. When you link your released faith with patience and persistence, you will have what it takes to tackle virtually any problem.

• •

When the way is rough, your patience has a chance to grow. So let it grow, and don't try to squirm out of your problems.

JAMES 1:3–4 TLB

• •

The secret of success is to be
like a duck——smooth and
unruffled on top, but paddling
furiously underneath.

• •

Wallace E. Johnson, president of Holiday
Inns and one of America's most successful
builders, once said, "I always keep a card in my
billfold with the following verses and refer to
them frequently: *Ask, and it shall be given you;
seek, and ye shall find; knock, and it shall be
opened unto you: for every one that asketh
receiveth; and he that seeketh findeth; and to him
that knocketh it shall be opened (Matthew 7:7–8).*

"These verses are among God's greatest promises. Yet they are a little one-sided. They indicate a
philosophy of receiving but not of giving. One
day as my wife, Alma, and I were seeking God's
guidance for a personal problem, I came across

the following verse which has since been a daily reminder to me of what my responsibility as a businessman is to God: *Study to shew thyself approved unto God, a workman that needeth not to be ashamed, rightly dividing the word of truth (2 Timothy 2:15).*

"Since then I have measured my actions against the phrase: *A workman that needeth not to be ashamed.*"

FAITH ON THE INSIDE + WORKS ON THE OUTSIDE = A SUCCESSFUL LIFE!

• •

I laboured more abundantly than
they all: yet not I, but the grace
of God which was with me.

1 CORINTHIANS 15:10

....

The cheerful man will do more in
the same time, will do it better,
will preserve it longer,
than the sad or sullen.

....

A little boy was once overheard talking to
himself as he strutted out of his house into the
backyard, carrying a baseball and bat. Once in
the yard, he tipped his baseball cap to his eager
puppy; and picking up the bat and ball, he
announced with a loud voice, "I'm the greatest
hitter in the world!"

He then proceeded to toss the ball into the
air, swing at it, and miss. "Strike one!" he cried,
as if playing the role of umpire.

He picked up the ball, threw it into the air, and
said again, "I'm the greatest baseball hitter ever!"
Again he swung at the ball and missed. "Strike
two!" he announced to his dog and the yard.

Undaunted, he picked up the ball, examined his bat, and then just before tossing the ball into the air, announced once again, "I'm the greatest hitter who ever lived!" He swung the bat hard but missed the ball for the third time. "Strike three!" he cried. Then he added, "Wow! What a pitcher! I'm the greatest pitcher in all the world!"

A positive mental attitude goes a long way toward making a difficult job seem small.

• •

When a man is gloomy, everything seems to go wrong; when he is cheerful, everything seems right!

PROVERBS 15:15 TLB

Money is a good servant
but a bad master.

At the age of twenty-four, financial advisor and author Ron Blue felt he had everything he needed to be successful—an MBA degree, a CPA certificate, and a prestigious position in the New York City office of the world's largest CPA firm. Then at the age of thirty-two, he committed his life to Jesus Christ and began to see life from a new perspective. When he decided to establish his own financial advisory firm, he used his skills to develop a business plan and arrange for a ten-thousand-dollar line of credit at a bank. Almost immediately, however, he felt convicted that God did not want him to borrow money to start his business. He canceled the credit line, not knowing what to do next but knowing he was not to go into debt.

One day, while explaining his business idea to a friend, the friend said, "Would you consider designing a financial seminar for our executives who are getting ready to retire?" Ron jumped at the opportunity. His friend was the training director for a large company, and the company agreed to pay six thousand dollars in advance for development of the seminar, then one thousand dollars each for four seminars during the year. Ron had the ten thousand dollars he needed without borrowing a dime.

Do your best to stay out of debt. You'll feel much freer, and God will bless you for trusting in Him.

• •

The rich ruleth over the poor, and
the borrower is servant to the lender.

PROVERBS 22:7

> No plan is worth the paper
> it is printed on unless it
> starts you doing something.

Nelson Diebel, a hyperactive and delinquent child, was enrolled in The Peddie School where he met swimming coach, Chris Martin, who believed the more one practices, the better one performs. Within a month, he had Nelson swimming thirty to forty hours a week, even though Nelson could not sit still in a classroom for fifteen minutes. Martin saw potential in Nelson. He constantly put new goals in front of the boy, trying to get him to focus and turn his anger into strength. Nelson eventually qualified for the Junior Nationals, and his fast times qualified him for Olympic Trials.

Then Nelson broke both hands and arms in a diving accident, and doctors warned he probably would never regain his winning form. Martin said to him, "You're coming all the way back. . . . If you're not committed to that, we're going to stop right now." Nelson agreed, and within weeks after his casts were off, he was swimming again.

In 1992, Nelson Diebel won an Olympic gold medal. As he accepted his medal, he recalls thinking: *I planned and dreamed and worked so hard, and I did it!* The kid who once couldn't sit still and who had no ambition had learned to make a plan, pursue it, and achieve it. He had become a winner in far more than swimming!

Let your plans motivate you to start working toward your goals. Dream big dreams!

• •

Be ye doers of the word, and not hearers
only, deceiving your own selves.

JAMES 1:22

> Life is a coin. You can spend
> it any way you wish, but
> you can spend it only once.

Frank, the head and founder of a major contracting firm, refused to celebrate the holidays, saying only, "Christmas is for children." Then one brisk December day, Frank was walking to work and was drawn to a Nativity scene in a department store window. He saw the Child anew. As he started to move away, a sign across the street caught his attention: "Holy Innocents Home." His mind raced back to a Sunday school lesson years ago about how King Herod had feared the baby Jesus and slaughtered children in Bethlehem. He recalled the day his own son, David, had died at the age of eighteen months. He had not been able to speak his name since.

Impulsively, Frank visited the library and was surprised to learn that Herod's men were estimated to have killed twenty children. He left the library with a mission. Later that night, he told his wife, Adele, that he had visited the orphanage and that he had given money for the building of a new wing. Then he said, "They are going to name it for David." What Frank did not tell his wife was that he had had a vision of twenty children playing in a bright new wing at Holy Innocents. As Adele hugged him, the vision came again, but this time, there were twenty-one children at play.

Don't miss the opportunity to spend your life on something worthwhile. You may have several opportunities, some big and some small, but none of them will be insignificant.

● ●

It is appointed unto men once to die,
but after this the judgment.

HEBREWS 9:27

Only passions, great passions,
can elevate the soul to great things.

The German sculptor, Dannaker, worked for
two years on a statue of Christ until it looked
perfect to him. He called a little girl into his
studio, and pointing to the statue, he asked her,
"Who is that?" The little girl promptly replied, "A
great man."

Dannaker was disheartened. He took his
chisel and began anew. For six long years, he
toiled. Again, he invited a little girl into his workshop, stood her before the figure, and said, "Who
is that?" She looked up at it for a moment, and
then tears welled up in her eyes as she folded her
hands across her chest and said, *Suffer the little
children to come unto me (Mark 10:14).* This time
Dannaker knew he had succeeded.

The sculptor later confessed that during
those six years, Christ had revealed Himself to

him in a vision, and he had only transferred to the marble what he had seen with his inner eyes.

Later, when Napoleon Bonaparte asked him to make a statue of Venus for the Louvre, Dannaker refused. "A man," he said, "who had seen Christ can never employ his gifts in carving a pagan goddess. My art is henceforth a consecrated thing."

The true value of a work comes not from effort, nor its completion, but from Christ who inspires it.

• •

Fervent in spirit; serving the Lord.

ROMANS 12:11

• •

Failures want pleasing methods,
successes want pleasing results.

• •

Sadie Delaney's father taught her always to strive to do better than her competition. She proved the value of that lesson shortly before she received her teaching license. A supervisor came to watch her and two other student teachers. Their assignment was to teach a class to bake cookies. Since the supervisor didn't have time for each teacher to go through the entire lesson, she divided the lesson, and Sadie was assigned to teach the girls how to serve and clean up.

The first student teacher panicked and forgot to halve the recipe and preheat the oven. The second girl was so behind because of the first girl's errors that the students made a mess in forming and baking the cookies. Then it was Sadie's turn. She said to the girls, "Listen, we have to work together as a team." They quickly baked the remaining dough. Several girls were lined up to scrub pans as soon as the cookies came out of the oven. Within ten minutes, they had several dozen perfect cookies and a clean kitchen. The supervisor was so impressed, she offered Sadie a substitute teacher's license on the spot. Sadie soon became the first black person ever to teach domestic science in New York City's public high schools.

Even when you have every right to blame others who have gone before you, don't make excuses. Do what it takes to get the job done!

● ●

No discipline seems pleasant at the time, but painful. Later on, however, it produces a harvest of righteousness and peace for those who have been trained by it.

HEBREWS 12:11 NIV

• •

Once a word has been allowed
to escape, it cannot be recalled.

• •

A man once sat down to have dinner with
his family. Before they began to eat, the family
members joined hands around the table, and the
man said a prayer, thanking God for the food, the
hands that had prepared it, and for the source of
all life. During the meal, however, he complained
at length about the staleness of the bread, the bitterness of the coffee, and a bit of mold he found
on one edge of the brick of cheese.

His young daughter asked him, "Daddy, do you
think God heard you say grace before the meal?"

"Of course, honey," he answered confidently.

Then she asked, "Do you think God heard
everything that was said during dinner?" The
man answered, "Why, yes, I believe so. God
hears everything."

She thought for a moment and then asked, "Daddy, which do you think God believed?"

The Lord hears everything we say during a day, not only those words that are addressed specifically to Him. Once you've said something, you can't take it back. Would you mind if God listened in on your conversations?

• •

Let no corrupt communication proceed out
of your mouth, but that which is good
to the use of edifying, that it may
minister grace unto the hearers.

EPHESIANS 4:29

Most of the things worth doing
in the world had been declared
impossible before they were done.

Consider these examples of resistance to ideas and inventions that we now consider commonplace:

1. In Germany, experts proved that if trains went as fast as fifteen miles an hour—considered a frightful speed—blood would spurt from the travelers' noses and passengers would suffocate when going through tunnels. In the United States, experts said the introduction of the railroad would require the building of many insane asylums since people would be driven mad with terror at the sight of the locomotives.

2. The New York YWCA announced typing lessons for women in 1881, and vigorous protest erupted on the grounds that the

female constitution would break down under the strain.

3. When the idea of iron ships was proposed, experts insisted that they would not float, would damage more easily than wooden ships when grounding, that it would be difficult to preserve the iron bottom from rust, and that iron would play havoc with compass readings.

4. New Jersey farmers resisted the first successful cast-iron plow invented in 1797, claiming that the cast iron would poison the land and stimulate the growth of weeds.

Don't let the word *impossible* stop you. If inventors and visionaries left every impossible task undone, our lives would be considerably more difficult. Nothing worth doing is impossible with the help of God!

• •

With God all things are possible.

MATTHEW 19:26

······································

*Obstacles are those frightful
things you see when you
take your eyes off the goal.*

······································

During the darkest days of the Civil War,
the hopes of the Union nearly died. When certain
goals seemed unreachable, the leaders of the
Union turned to President Abraham Lincoln for
solace, guidance, and encouragement. Once when
a delegation called at the White House and
detailed a long list of crises facing the nation,
Lincoln told this story:

"Years ago a young friend and I were out one
night when a shower of meteors fell from the
clear November sky. The young man was frightened, but I told him to look up in the sky past
the shooting stars to the fixed stars beyond,
shining serene in the firmament, and I said, 'Let
us not mind the meteors, but let us keep our eyes
on the stars.'"

When times are troubled or life seems to be changing too fast, keep your inner eyes of faith and hope on those things that you know to be lasting and sure. Don't limit your gaze to what you know or who you know, but focus on whom you know. God alone—and a relationship with Him that is eternal—is the supreme goal. He never changes, and He cannot be removed from His place as the King of Glory.

• •

Peter . . . walked on the water toward Jesus.
But when he looked around at the high waves,
he was terrified and began to sink.

MATTHEW 14:29–30 TLB

A good reputation is
more valuable than money.

In *Up from Slavery,* Booker T. Washington
describes meeting an ex-slave from Virginia:

"I found that this man had made a contract
with his master, two or three years previous to
the Emancipation Proclamation, to the effect that
the slave was to be permitted to buy himself, by
paying so much per year for his body; and while
he was paying for himself, he was to be permitted
to labor where and for whom he pleased.

"Finding that he could secure better
wages in Ohio, he went there. When
freedom came, he was still in debt to his
master some 300 dollars. Notwithstanding
that the Emancipation Proclamation
freed him from any obligation to his
master, this black man walked the greater
portion of the distance back to where his

old master lived in Virginia, and placed the last dollar, with interest, in his hands.

"In talking to me about this, the man told me that he knew that he did not have to pay his debt, but that he had given his word to his master, and his word he had never broken. He felt that he could not enjoy his freedom till he had fulfilled his promise."

Your ability to keep your word, not your ability to acquire money, is your true measure as a person!

A good name is rather to be
chosen than great riches.

PROVERBS 22:1

> An error doesn't become a mistake
> until you refuse to correct it.

A janitor at the First Security Bank in Boise, Idaho, once accidentally put a box of eight thousand checks worth $840,000 on a trash table. That night, the operator of the paper shredder dutifully dumped the box of checks into his machine, which cut the checks into quarter-inch shreds. He then dumped the paper scraps into a garbage can outside the bank. When the bank supervisor realized what happened the next morning, he wanted to cry.

Most of the checks had been cashed at the bank and were awaiting shipment to a clearinghouse. Their loss represented a bookkeeping nightmare since most of the checks were still unrecorded, and as a result, the bankers could not know who paid what to whom.

What did the supervisor do? He ordered that the shredded pieces be reconstructed. Fifty employees worked in two shifts for six hours a day inside six rooms—shifting, matching, and pasting the pieces together as if they were jigsaw puzzles—until all eight thousand of the checks were put together again.

Humpty Dumpty may have fallen from the wall, but did the king's men even try to put him together again? If you make a mistake, work on a solution!

● ●

He who heeds discipline shows the
way to life, but whoever ignores
correction leads others astray.

PROVERBS 10:17 NIV

• •

Hating people is like burning down
your own house to get rid of a rat.

• •

After two years in the navy, Willard Scott
returned to his old job with NBC radio, but to a
new supervisor. Willard found himself at odds
with his new boss at every turn, and he was furious
when he rescheduled *Joy Boys,* a comedy show
Willard did with Eddie Walker, for the worst slot
on radio—eight to midnight. Willard was braced
for a change-or-I'll-leave confrontation when he
recalled Proverbs 19:11 NIV—*A man's wisdom
gives him patience; it is to his glory to overlook an
offense.* He and Eddie decided to work themselves
to the bone, and within three years, they made
Joy Boys the top-rated show in Washington.

Willard says, "I learned that I, too, had been
wrong. In all my dealings with my boss, I had
aggravated the problem. I knew he didn't like me,
and in response I was barely civil to him and

dodged him as much as I could; but one day he invited me to a station party I couldn't avoid. There I met his fiancée. She was bright, alive, and down-to-earth. *How could a woman like that care for anybody who didn't have something to recommend him?* I was able to get new insight into my boss's character. As time went on my attitude changed, and so did his." Willard and his boss became friends, and he remained at NBC.

Is there someone with whom you are at odds? If you're looking for the negative qualities in a person, you're sure to find them. Try seeing them with new eyes. A fresh perspective can change everything.

• •

If ye bite and devour one another, take heed that ye be not consumed one of another.

GALATIANS 5:15

Laughter is the sun that drives winter from the human face.

A missionary from Sweden was once urged by his friends to give up his idea of returning to India because it was so hot there. "Man," the fellow Swede urged, as if telling his friend something he didn't already know, "it's 120 degrees in the shade in that country!" The Swedish missionary replied "Vell, ve don't alvays have to stay in the shade do ve?"

Humor is not a sin. It is a God-given escape hatch. Being able to see the lighter side of life is a virtue. Every vocation and circumstance of life has a lighter side, if we are only willing to see it. Wholesome humor can do a great deal to help defuse a tense, heated situation. In developing a good sense of humor, we must be able to laugh at our own mistakes; accept justified criticism and recover from it; and learn to avoid using statements that are unsuitable, even though they may be funny.

James M. Gray and William Houghton—two Godly men—were praying together one day, and the elderly Dr. Gray concluded his prayer by saying, "Lord, keep me cheerful. Keep me from becoming a cranky, old man."

Keeping a sense of humor is a great way to become a sweet, patient, and encouraging person. Learn to laugh at yourself occasionally!

• •

A merry heart maketh a cheerful
countenance: but by sorrow of
the heart the spirit is broken.

PROVERBS 15:13

Good nature begets smiles,
smiles beget friends, and friends
are better than a fortune.

It has been estimated that more than ninety-five percent of all Americans receive at least one or more Christmas cards each year. The average is actually more than seventy cards per family! Millions of cards are mailed worldwide each holiday season. Have you ever wondered where this custom began?

A museum director in the mid-nineteenth century had a personal habit of sending notes to his friends at Christmastime each year, just to wish them a joyful holiday season. One year, he found he had little time to write, yet he still wanted to send a message of good cheer. He asked his friend, John Horsely, to design a card that he might sign and send. Those who received the cards loved them so much they created cards of their own. Thus the Christmas card was invented!

It's often the simple heartfelt gestures in life that speak most loudly of friendship. Ask yourself today, *What can I do to bring a smile to the face of a friend? What can I do to bring good cheer into the life of someone who is in need, trouble, sickness, or sorrow?* Follow through on your answer. It's not a gift you are giving as much as a friendship you are building!

• •

The light in the eyes [of him whose heart is joyful] rejoices the hearts of others.

PROVERBS 15:30 AMP

· ·

No person was ever honored for
what he received. Honor has been
the reward for what he gave.

· ·

This American received a medical degree
from New York University College of Medicine.
He received an appointment to the Virus
Research Laboratory at the University of
Pittsburgh. He received an assignment from the
army to develop a vaccine against influenza, and
among the many honors he received was a
Presidential Medal of Freedom.

Jonas Salk, however, is not known for what
he received, but for what he gave. He and his
team of researchers gave their efforts to prepare
an inactivated polio virus that could serve as an
immunizing agent against polio. By 1952, they
had created a vaccine; and in 1955, the vaccine
was released for widespread use in the United

States, virtually ending the ravaging, crippling effects of polio.

You will receive many opportunities in your life and most likely, a number of certificates, diplomas, and awards. What ultimately will count, however, is what you do with the training you have received and the skills and traits you have developed.

Find a way to give, create, or generate something today that will benefit others. In your actions will be not only a potential for fame and reward, but also great personal satisfaction—the reward of highest value.

• •

The righteous give without sparing.

PROVERBS 21:26 NIV

• •

The difference between the
right word and the almost right
word is the difference between
lightning and the lightning bug.

• •

Consider the infamous statements listed
below, and notice as you read that they all could be
corrected by changing or inserting only one word!

"Everything that can be invented has been
invented."—Charles H. Duell, U.S. Patent Office
director, 1899

"Who wants to hear actors talk?"—H.M.
Warner, Warner Brothers Pictures 1927

"Sensible and responsible women do not
want to vote."—Grover Cleveland, 1905

"There is no likelihood man can ever tap the
power of the atom."—Robert Millikan, Nobel
Prize winner in physics, 1923

"Heavier-than-air flying machines are impossible."—Lord Kelvin, president, Royal Society, 1895

"[Babe] Ruth made a big mistake when he gave up pitching."—Tris Speaker, 1927

Gone with the Wind is going to be the biggest flop in Hollywood history."—Gary Cooper

Isn't it amazing what a difference a word or two can make! Choose your words carefully. Always think before you speak.

• •

A word fitly spoken is like apples

of gold in pictures of silver.

PROVERBS 25:11

This world belongs to the man
who is wise enough to change
his mind in the presence of facts.

A feud developed between two families who
lived side by side in the mountains of Kentucky.
It started when Grandpa Smith's cow jumped a
stone fence and ate Grandpa Brown's corn.
Brown shot the cow. A Smith boy then shot *two*
Brown boys. The Browns shot one Smith. Bill
Brown planned to kill a second Smith, but before
he could, he was called away to war. While he was
away, Bill's mother had a hard time making ends
meet for her family, since Bill's father had been
one of the victims.

At Christmas, the head of the Smith clan
took his family to church. Usually he stayed
outside, but this year it was so cold he went in to
wait. The sermon was on Christ, the Prince of
Peace, who died in *our* place for *our* sins. It

struck him hard. He realized what a crime he had committed, repented, and then secretly hired a young boy to carry a basket of food to the Brown's home every day until Bill returned.

Once home, Bill set out to discover who had so generously helped his family. He followed the boy to the Smith's house, where Smith met him and said, "Shoot me, Bill, if you want to. But Christ has already died for my sins, and I hope you'll forgive me too." Bill did, and neighbors truly became neighbors again.

Never reach the point in life where you think you can't learn something new or change your opinion about something. You are never too old, or too young, to be forgiven.

• •

Whoever heeds correction

gains understanding.

PROVERBS 15:32 NIV

Do not remove a fly from your friend's forehead with a hatchet.

One day, a young altar boy was serving the priest at a Sunday Mass being held in the country church of his small village. The boy, nervous in his new role at the altar, accidentally dropped the cruet of wine. The village priest immediately struck the boy sharply on the cheek and in a very gruff voice, shouted so that many people could hear, "Leave the altar and don't come back!" That boy became Tito, the Communist leader who ruled Yugoslavia for many decades.

One day in a large city cathedral, a young boy was serving a bishop at a Sunday Mass. He, too, accidentally dropped the cruet of wine. The bishop turned to him but rather than responding in anger, gently whispered with a warm twinkle in his eyes, "Someday you will be a priest." That boy grew up to become Archbishop Fulton Sheen.

Words have power. The childhood phrase, "Sticks and stones can break my bones, but words can never hurt me," simply isn't true. Words do hurt. They wound—sometimes deeply.

Words also can reward, build self-esteem, create friendships, give hope, and render a blessing. Words can heal and drive accomplishment.

Watch what you say to a friend today! Are your words like poison to the heart, or do they drip with the sweetness of honey?

• •

Reprove, rebuke, exhort, with
great patience and instruction.

2 TIMOTHY 4:2 NASB

Every calling is great
when greatly pursued.

A farmer once caught a young eagle in the forest, brought it home, and raised it among his ducks and turkeys. Five years later, a naturalist came to visit him and saw the bird. "That's an eagle not a chicken!" he said. "Yes," said the farmer, "but I've raised it to be a chicken." "Still," said the naturalist, "it has a wingspan of fifteen feet. It's an eagle!" "It will never fly," said the farmer. The naturalist disagreed, and they decided to put their argument to the test.

First, the naturalist picked up the eagle and said, "Eagle, thou art an eagle; thou dost belong to the sky and not to this earth; stretch forth thy wings and fly." The eagle saw the chickens and jumped down. The next day, the naturalist took the eagle to the top of the house and said the same thing before letting the eagle go. Again, it spotted the chickens below and fluttered down to join them in feeding.

"One more try," said the naturalist. He took the eagle up a mountain. The trembling bird looked around, and then the naturalist made it look into the sun. Suddenly, the eagle stretched out its wings, gave a mighty screech, and flew away, never to return.

People may say you are just a hunk of flesh—a chicken rather than an eagle. But deep inside, you have a spirit created in God's image, and you are destined to fly.

• •

I press toward the mark for the prize of
the high calling of God in Christ Jesus.

PHILIPPIANS 3:14

Treat everybody alike, no matter
from what station in life he comes. . . .
Really great men and women are
those who are natural, frank,
and honest with everyone with
whom they come into contact.

In ancient Greece, the philosopher
Aristippus—considered by all who knew him to
be the master of political craftiness—learned to
get along well in royal circles by flattering the
tyrant Denys. Not only did he flatter Denys, but
he was proud that he did. In fact, Aristippus dis-
dained less prosperous fellow philosophers and
wise men who refused to stoop that low.

One day, Aristippus saw his colleague
Diogenes washing vegetables, and he said to him,
"If you would only learn to flatter King Denys,
you would not have to be washing lentils."

Diogenes looked up slowly and replied, "And you, if you had only learned to live on lentils, would not have to flatter King Denys."

Another way to regard flattery is this:

F—foolish

L—laughable

A—accolades

T—to

T—tell

E—everyone

R—'round

Y—you

Speak the truth sincerely. When the truth is painful, consider the option of remaining silent!

• •

Don't show favoritism.

JAMES 2:1 NIV

'Tis better to be alone,
than in bad company.

Coach Gregory watched with pride as
Rashaan Salaam accepted the Heisman Trophy.
He recalled the hotshot eighteen-year-old who,
finally free from his mother's tight discipline, had
arrived in Colorado ready to devour the world.
He said, "Rashaan was a gangster wannabe. He
came here wearing all this red stuff, talking about
gangs. He hadn't done it back home because his
mother would never have tolerated it." Neither
did Gregory. He never lectured or preached to
Rashaan, but he did ask him questions. When
Rashaan came to him, talking about his new
friends, Gregory said, "Sure, they are your
friends, but are you their friend? They know what
you're trying to accomplish. They know the
potential you have to do great things. If you are
their friend, when they get ready to get into

something, they'll say, 'Salaam, get out of here. Go home and study.'"

As a coach, Gregory wanted Salaam to find daylight and get into the end zone; but as his friend, he wanted him to live in the daylight and make it to life's goal line as a productive citizen. Winning a football game is never a one-man effort. It's a team effort. The same holds true for life, and the good news is you can choose the players on your team!

• •

Do not be misled: "Bad company

corrupts good character."

1 CORINTHIANS 15:33 NIV

The rotten apple spoils
his companion.

In his book *The Mind of Watergate,* psychiatrist Leo Rangell, M.D., relates what he calls a "compromise of integrity" as he analyzes the relationship between former President Richard M. Nixon and several of his closest confidants. He records a conversation between investigative committee member Senator Howard Baker and young Herbert L. Porter:

Baker: "Did you ever have any qualms about what you were doing? Did you ever think of saying, 'I do not think this is quite right.' Did you ever think of that?"

Porter: "Yes, I did."

Baker: "What did you do about it?"

Porter: "I did not do anything."

Baker: "Why didn't you?"

Porter: "In all honesty, probably because of the fear of the group pressure that would ensue, of not being a team player."

There's nothing wrong with being a team player as long as you choose the right team! You will become like your friends, even as they change and become a little more like you. Therefore, choose your friends cautiously and thoughtfully.

• •

He that walketh with wise men shall be wise: but a companion of fools shall be destroyed.

PROVERBS 13:20

Patience is bitter but its fruit is sweet.

We often think of great artists and musicians as having bursts of genius. More often, they are models of painstaking patience. Their greatest works tend to have been accomplished over long periods and in extreme hardships.

Beethoven is said to have rewritten each bar of his music at least a dozen times.

Josef Haydn produced more than eight hundred musical compositions before writing *The Creation*, the oratorio for which he is most famous.

Michelangelo's *Last Judgment* is considered one of the twelve master paintings of the ages. It took him eight years to complete. He produced more than two thousand sketches and renderings in the process.

Leonardo da Vinci worked on *The Last Supper* for ten years, often working so diligently that he forgot to eat.

When he was quite elderly, the pianist Ignace Paderewski was asked by an admirer, "Is it true that you still practice every day?" He replied, "Yes, at least six hours a day." The admirer said in awe, "You must have a world of patience." Paderewski said, "I have no more patience than the next fellow. I just use mine."

Put your patience to use in the pursuit of your dreams.

• •

Ye have need of patience, that,

after ye have done the will of God,

ye might receive the promise.

HEBREWS 10:36

> Motivation is when your
> dreams put on work clothes.

In 1972, *Life* magazine published a story about the amazing adventures of John Goddard. When he was fifteen, John's grandmother said, "If only I had done that when I was young. . . ." Determined not to make that statement at the end of his life, John wrote out 127 goals for his life.

He named ten rivers he wanted to explore and seventeen mountains he wanted to climb. He set goals of becoming an Eagle Scout, a world traveler, and a pilot. Also on his list was: ride a horse in the Rose Bowl parade, dive in a submarine, retrace the travels of Marco Polo, read the Bible from cover to cover, and read the entire *Encyclopedia Britannica.*

He also planned to read the entire works of Shakespeare, Plato, Dickens, Socrates, Aristotle, and several other classic authors. He desired to learn to play the flute and violin, marry, have children (he had five), pursue a career in medicine, and serve as a missionary for his church.

Sound impossible? At the age of forty-seven, John Goddard had accomplished one hundred and three of his goals!

Your list of goals may not be as extensive as John Goddard's, but if you don't have *some* goals in life, you'll find that you have little motivation to get up in the morning and little satisfaction as your head hits the pillow each night.

• •

Whatever you do, work at it with all your heart, as working for the Lord, not for men.

COLOSSIANS 3:23 NIV

Not only to say the right thing in the right place, but far more difficult, to leave unsaid the wrong thing at the tempting moment.

William Penn, founding leader of the colony that became Pennsylvania, had these rules for conversation: "Avoid company where it is not profitable or necessary, and in those occasions, speak little, and last. Silence is wisdom where speaking is folly, and always safe. Some are so foolish as to interrupt and anticipate those that speak instead of hearing and thinking before they answer, which is uncivil, as well as silly. If thou thinkest twice before thou speakest once, thou wilt speak twice the better for it. Better to say nothing than not to the purpose. And to speak pertinently, consider both what is fit, and when it is fit, to speak. In all debates, let truth be thy aim, not victory or an unjust interest; and endeavor to gain, rather than to expose, thy antagonist."

A little girl named Mary had come home from a tough day at school. She stretched herself out on the living room sofa to have her own private pity party. She moaned to her mother and brother, "Nobody loves me . . . the whole world hates me!"

Her brother, busily occupied with his Nintendo, hardly looked her way as he passed on this encouraging word: "That's not true, Mary. Some people don't even know you."

Mary, no doubt, was not amused. She probably wished her brother had heeded the advice of William Penn. One of the greatest skills you can develop in life is the ability to control your tongue!

• •

Self-control means controlling the tongue!

A quick retort can ruin everything.

PROVERBS 13:3 TLB

School seeks to get you ready for examination; life gives the finals.

The Koh-in-noor diamond is among the world's most spectacular. It is part of the British crown jewels, presented to Queen Victoria by a maharajah in India when the maharajah was only a young boy.

Years later, when he was a grown man, the maharajah visited Queen Victoria in England. He asked that the stone be brought from the Tower of London, where it was kept in safety, to Buckingham Palace. The queen did as he requested.

Taking the diamond in his hand, he knelt before the queen and presented it back to her, saying, "Your Majesty, I gave this jewel when I was a child, too young to know what I was doing. I want to give it to you again in the fullness of my strength, with all of my heart and affection, and gratitude, now and forever, fully realizing all that I do."

A day will come when you likely will look back and say, "I'm grateful for my teachers and the lessons they taught me about discipline, concentration, hard work, cooperation, and the right and wrong ways to compete." Even more valuable will be the day when you look in a mirror and say, "Knowing what I now know about life, I see value in continuing to teach these lessons to myself."

• •

Examine yourselves to see whether
you are in the faith; test yourselves.

2 CORINTHIANS 13:5 NIV

· ·

Diligence is the mother
of good fortune.

· ·

The *Sixty-Four-Thousand-Dollar Question* was
the hottest show on television in 1955. The more
Joyce watched the program, the more she thought,
"I could do that." At the time, Joyce had quit her
teaching job to raise her daughter, and she and her
husband were living on fifty dollars a month. She
never dreamed of winning the top prize—*any*
prize at that point would have helped greatly.

As a psychologist by training, Joyce analyzed
the show. She saw that each contestant had a
built-in incongruity—the marine who was a
gourmet cook, the shoemaker who knew about
opera. She looked at herself. She was a short,
blond psychologist and mother with no incongruity. After some thought, she decided to
become an expert in boxing! She ate, drank, and
slept boxing, studying its statistics, personalities,

and history. When she felt she was ready, she applied as a contestant for the show, was accepted, won, and won again, until she eventually won the sixty-four-thousand-dollar prize.

That experience led her to dream of a career as a television journalist who might translate the results of psychological research into terms that people could use in their everyday lives. Once she saw that possibility, there was no stopping Dr. Joyce Brothers.

True success never comes by chance. Diligently apply yourself to your goals, and your dreams will come true.

• •

The plans of the diligent lead to profit.

PROVERBS 21:5 NIV

> The road to success is dotted with many tempting parking places.

The first thing to emerge at a baby giraffe's birth is its front hooves and head. Minutes later, the newborn is hurled from its mother's body, falls ten feet, and lands on its back. Within seconds, it rolls to an upright position with its legs tucked under its body. From this position, it views the world for the first time and shakes off any remaining birthing fluid.

The mother giraffe lowers her head just long enough to take a quick look at her calf, and then she does what seems to be a very unreasonable thing—she kicks her baby, sending it sprawling head over heels. If it doesn't get up, she kicks it again and again until the calf finally stands on its wobbly legs. Then what does the mother giraffe do? She kicks it off its feet! Why? She wants it to remember how to get up.

In the wild, baby giraffes must be able to get up as quickly as possible to stay with the herd and avoid becoming a meal for lions, hyenas, leopards, or wild hunting dogs. The best way a mother giraffe has of ensuring that her calf lives is for her to teach it to get up quickly and get with it.

Don't complain if those who love you push you into action when you'd rather be in park. They are doing you a favor.

● ●

Let us lay aside every weight, and the sin which doth so easily beset us, and let us run with patience the race that is set before us.

HEBREWS 12:1

When you are laboring for others
let it be with the same zeal
as if it were for yourself.

On May 21, 1946, a scientist at Los Alamos was carrying out a necessary experiment in preparation for an atomic test to be conducted in the waters of the South Pacific. He had successfully performed this experiment many times before. It involved pushing two hemispheres of uranium together to determine the amount of U-235 needed for a chain reaction—the amount scientists call "a critical mass." Just as the mass became critical, he would push the hemispheres apart with his screwdriver, instantly stopping the chain reaction.

That day, however, just as the material became critical, the screwdriver slipped. The hemispheres of uranium came too close together, and instantly, the room was filled with a dazzling bluish haze. Young Louis Soltin, instead of ducking and thereby possibly saving himself, tore the two hemispheres apart with his hands, thus interrupting the chain reaction.

In this instant, self-forgetful act, he saved the lives of seven other people who were in the room. He, however, died in agony nine days later.

Today, do something for someone else with the same energy you would use if you were doing it for yourself.

• •

Each of you should look not only
to your own interests, but also
to the interests of others.

PHILIPPIANS 2:4 NIV

The Bible knows nothing of a
hierarchy of labor. No work
is degrading. If it ought to
be done, then it is good work.

When David was twelve, he convinced a
restaurant manager that he was actually sixteen
and was hired as a lunch-counter waiter for
twenty-five cents an hour. The place was owned by
two Greek immigrant brothers, Frank and George,
who had started their lives in America as a dish-
washer and hot-dog seller. David remembers that
they set high standards and never asked anything
of their employees that they wouldn't do themselves. Frank once told David, "As long as you try,
you can always work for me. But when you don't
try, you can't work for me." Trying meant everything from working hard to treating customers
politely. Once, when Frank noticed a waitress

giving a customer a rough time, he fired her on the spot and waited on the table himself. David determined that would never happen to him.

The usual tip for waiters in those days was a dime, but David discovered that if he brought the food out quickly and was especially polite, he sometimes got a quarter as a tip. He set a goal for himself to see how many customers he could wait on in one night. His record was one hundred!

Today, R. David Thomas is better known as "Dave," the founder and senior chairman of Wendy's International, Inc., a chain of 4,300 restaurants.

No matter what job you do, do it well. The Bible tells us to do all our work *as to the Lord (Colossians 3:23).*

• •

To rejoice in his labour;
this is the gift of God.

ECCLESIASTES 5:19

• •

The ripest peach is
highest on the tree.

• •

McCormick's father was what many might
call a tinkerer. A mechanical genius, he invented
many farm devices. Sadly, however, he became
the laughingstock of his community for attempt-
ing to make a grain-cutting device. For years, he
worked on the project but never succeeded in
getting it to operate reliably.

In spite of the discouragement his father
experienced and the continuing ridicule of
neighbors, young McCormick took up the old
machine as his own project. He also experienced
years of experimentation and failure. Then one
day, he succeeded in constructing a reaper that
would harvest grain.

Even so, jealous opposition prevented the
invention from being used for a number of years.
McCormick was able to make sales only after he

gave a personal guarantee to each purchaser that the reaper would do the job he claimed it could do. Finally, after decades of trial and error, hoping and waiting, a firm in Cincinnati agreed to manufacture one hundred machines, and the famous McCormick reaper was born.

To get to the ripest peach on the highest branch, you need to climb one limb at a time and not be defeated by the scrape of bark, the occasional fall, and the frequent feeling of being left dangling!

• •

Let us not become weary in doing good, for at the proper time we will reap a harvest if we do not give up.

GALATIANS 6:9 NIV

When you do the things you have to do when you have to do them, the day will come when you can do the things you want to do when you want to do them.

The bee is often described as being busy. It deserves this adjective! To produce one pound of honey, a bee must visit 56,000 clover heads. Since each head has sixty flower tubes, a bee must make a total of 3,360,000 visits. In the process, the average bee would travel the equivalent of three times around the world.

To make just one *tablespoon* of honey, the amount that might go on a biscuit, a little bee must make 4,200 trips to the flowers, averaging about ten trips a day, each trip lasting approximately twenty minutes. It visits four hundred different flowers.

Day in, day out, the work of a bee is fairly unglamorous. It flies, it takes in nectar, it flies some more, and it deposits nectar. In the process, it produces, and what it produces creates a place for it in the hive.

You may think your daily chores are a waste of time; but in fact, your completion of those chores is making you. One day, you won't even have to think: *I must get disciplined. I must get to work. I must stick with it.* If you have done your chores faithfully and to the best of your ability, the chores will have become a part of the way you tackle every challenge the rest of your life.

• •

He becometh poor that dealeth
with a slack hand: but the hand
of the diligent maketh rich.

PROVERBS 10:4

> A man without mirth is like
> a wagon without springs,
> he is jolted disagreeably by
> every pebble in the road.

Dr. Ashley Montagu met two young men shortly after the end of World War II. They had spent two years in Auschwitz, the cruel death camp operated by the Nazis. Prior to Auschwitz, they had lived in Vienna in a cellar where they had been kept hidden by Christian friends. All of the others housed with them in the cellar had been exterminated solely because they were Jews. After the war ended, these two men had walked from Vienna to Berlin, hoping to find relatives. There, they were picked up by an American Jewish soldier who brought them to America. Both of them wanted to become physicians; and that's how Dr. Montagu, a professor in a medical school, came to meet them. Noting that they "didn't exhibit any of the scars that one might have expected from their unhappy existence," he asked them how they came to be such cheerful people.

They replied, "A group of us decided that no matter what happened, it wouldn't get us down." They told him they had attempted to be cheerful regardless of their circumstances, never yielding for a moment to the idea that they were either inferior or doomed.

They were living proof to Dr. Montagu that even under impossible conditions, it's possible to be happy!

• •

A merry heart doeth good like a medicine:
but a broken spirit drieth the bones.

PROVERBS 17:22

The two most important words: "Thank you." The most important word: "We." The least important word: "I."

• •

There's an old saying that goes, "It needs more skill than I can tell, to play the second fiddle well."

Along that line, Leonard Bernstein was once asked which instrument was the most difficult to play. He thought for a moment and said, "The second fiddle. I can get plenty of first violinists, but to find someone who can play the second fiddle with enthusiasm—that's a problem. And if we have no second fiddle, we have no harmony."

General Robert E. Lee was a man who knew the value of playing second fiddle. This great general never stopped being a true southern gentleman. Once, while riding on a train to Richmond, he was seated at the rear of the car. All the other places were filled with officers and soldiers. A poorly dressed, elderly woman boarded the coach at a rural station, and finding no seat offered to her, she trudged down the aisle toward the back of the car. Immediately, Lee stood up and offered her his place. One after another of the men then arose and offered the general his seat. "No, gentlemen," he replied, "if there is none for this lady, there can be none for me!"

Genuine humility is what prompts us to offer a heartfelt thank you and to favor others over ourselves.

• •

Don't be selfish. . . . Be humble, thinking of others as better than yourself.

PHILIPPIANS 2:3 TLB

Here's the key to success and
the key to failure: we become
what we think about.

A number of years ago the John Hancock
Mutual Life Insurance Company ran an ad that said:

> "There was once a man who loved
> nature with such a deep and moving love
> that she told him one of her secrets. She
> gave him the power to create new plants.
> The man, whose name was Luther
> Burbank, . . . saw that every plant was a
> child. It had its own face, own promise,
> its unique touch of genius or character.
> And if that promise were tended and
> encouraged, the plant would grow more
> useful and beautiful each year. Luther
> Burbank . . . made potatoes grow larger,
> whiter, more delicious than they had ever
> been. He taught the cactus of the desert
> to throw away its spines, so that cattle

could fatten upon it, and made the black-berry shed its thorns, so it would not cut the fingers of the pickers. For him, the plum grew without pits, and strawberries ripened all year . . . he left the earth covered with flowers and fruits that no one had ever attempted to grow before. And all because he knew a secret. He knew that everything that lives has the power to become greater."

Choose to see new possibilities. Put your mind to them. Let them be the focus of your thoughts, and then pursue them! You will become greater for it.

● ●

Finally, brethren, whatsoever things are true, whatsoever things are honest, . . . if there be any virtue, and if there be any praise, think on these things.

PHILIPPIANS 4:8

Always bear in mind that your own
resolution to success is more important
than any other one thing.

Famous stage and film actress Helen Hayes
believed her resoluteness about her own potential
for success played an important role at the beginning of her career. She once told the story of a
particular audition: "Before the authors gave me
the script, they observed, in a matter-of-course
manner, 'Of course you play piano? You'll have to
sing to your own accompaniment in the piece.' As
these alarming tidings were in the course of
being made, I caught a bewildered look in my
mother's eyes, and so I spoke up before she
could. 'Certainly I play piano,' I answered.

"As we left the theater, my mother sighed, 'I
hate to see you start under a handicap,' she said.
'What made you say you could play piano?' 'The
feeling that I will play before rehearsals begin,' I

said. We went at once to try to rent a piano and ended by buying one. I began lessons at once, practiced finger exercises till I could no longer see the notes—and began rehearsals with the ability to accompany myself. Since then, I have never lived too far from a piano."

What you believe about your own potential for success counts far more than what any other person may believe. Believe what God believes about you—you were created for success.

• •

The Lord GOD will help me; therefore
shall I not be confounded: therefore
have I set my face like a flint, and
I know that I shall not be ashamed.

ISAIAH 50:7

• 253 •

Triumph is just "umph" added to try.

Many years ago in England, a small boy grew up speaking with a lisp. He was never a scholar in school. When war broke out involving his nation, he was rejected from service, told that "we need *men*." He once rose to address the House of Commons, and all present walked out of the room. In fact, he often spoke to empty chairs and echoes. One day, he became prime minister of Great Britain; and with stirring speeches and bold decisions, he led his nation to victory. His name was Sir Winston Churchill.

Many years ago in Illinois, a man with only a few years of formal education failed in business in '31, was defeated in a run for the state legislature in '32, again failed in business in '33, was elected to the legislature in '34, but was defeated for speaker in '38. He was defeated for elector in

'40, defeated for Congress in '43, elected to Congress in '46, but defeated in '48. He was defeated for Senate in '55, defeated for the vice-presidential nomination in '56, and defeated for the Senate in '58. In 1860, however, he was elected president. His name was Abraham Lincoln.

No one is defeated until he gives up trying.

• •

Whatsoever thy hand findeth
to do, do it with thy might.

ECCLESIASTES 9:10

> A goal properly set is
> halfway reached.

A young man in need of work once saw this advertisement in a Boston newspaper: "Wanted: young man as an understudy to a financial statistician, P.O. Box 1720." The young man decided this was just the kind of job he wanted, so he replied to the ad but received no answer. He wrote again and even a third time with no reply. Next, he went to the Boston post office and asked the name of the holder of Box 1720, but the clerk refused to give it, as did the postmaster.

Early one morning, an idea came to the young man. He rose early, took the first train to Boston, went to the post office, and stood watch near Box 1720. After a while, a man appeared, opened the box, and took out the mail. The young man followed him as he returned to the office of a stock brokerage firm. The young man entered and asked for the manager.

In the interview, the manager asked, "How did you find out that I was the advertiser?" The young man told about his detective work, to which the manager replied, "Young man, you are just the kind of persistent fellow I want. You are employed!"

If a goal is worthy, there's no good reason to stop pursuing it! Find something you truly want to do, then go for it with all your heart, mind, and strength.

• •

The LORD answered me, and said,
Write the vision, and make it plain upon
tables, that he may run that readeth it.

HABAKKUK 2:2

> I think the one lesson I have
> learned is that there is no
> substitute for paying attention.

Henry P. Davison was a prominent American financier and one-time head of the American Red Cross. He worked his way up from being a poor boy to become president of a large New York City bank.

While he was a cashier of that bank, a would-be robber came to his window, pointed a revolver at him, and passed a check across his window counter. The check was for one million dollars, payable to the Almighty. Davison remained calm, even though he realized the gravity of the situation. In a loud voice, he repeated the words on the check back to the person standing in front of him, emphasizing the "million dollars." Then he graciously asked the would-be robber how he would like to have *the million dollars* for the

Almighty. He then proceeded to count out small bills. In the meantime, the suspicion of a guard had been aroused by the strange request he had overheard. He disarmed the robber and prevented the theft.

In later years, Davison was often asked to give his wisdom to others seeking success. He often advised that courtesy, readiness, willingness, and alertness do more for a person than just being smart.

It has been said that one of the skills of a good communicator is the ability to listen. Paying attention to the words and actions of those around you may be the best schooling you'll ever receive.

• •

We ought to give the more earnest heed

to the things which we have heard,

lest at any time we should let them slip.

HEBREWS 2:1

> A good listener is not only
> popular everywhere, but after
> a while he knows something.

An American Indian was once visiting New York City; and as he walked the busy Manhattan streets with a friend from the city, he suddenly stopped, tilted his head to one side, and said, "I hear a cricket."

"You're crazy," his friend said. The Cherokee answered, "No, I hear a cricket. I do! I'm sure of it."

The friend replied, "It's the noon hour. People are jammed on the sidewalks, cars are honking, taxis are whizzing by, the city is full of noise. And you think you can hear a cricket?"

"I'm sure I do," said the visitor. He listened even more closely and then walked to the corner, spotted a shrub in a large cement planter, dug into the leaves underneath it, and pulled out a cricket. His friend was astounded. The man said, "The fact is, my friend, that my ears are different than yours. It all depends on what your ears have been tuned to hear. Let me show you." At that, he reached into his pocket, pulled out a handful of loose change, and dropped the coins on the pavement. Every head within a half block turned. "See what I mean?" he said, picking up the coins. "It all depends on what you are listening for."

Listen today to those things that will make you wise. Don't neglect those things that will prepare you for eternity.

•••••••••••••••••••••••••••••••

The ear that heareth the reproof
of life abideth among the wise.

PROVERBS 15:31

You may be disappointed if you fail, but you are doomed if you don't try.

These words were spelled out in lights at the 18th Olympics in Tokyo: "The most important thing in the Olympic Games is not to win but to take part; just as the most important thing in life is not the triumph but the struggle. The essential thing is . . . to have fought well."

The athletes who make it to the Olympic Games are already the best of the best from each nation. Each athlete has excelled in ways few of his or her peers will ever reach. Yet only one will wear a gold medal, one a silver, and one a bronze. Those who are so accustomed to winning face the devastating possibility of losing before not only their teammates, but also their countrymen, and, in this age of worldwide television, before the entire world. How vital it is for these athletes to keep their perspective—

that winning is not the important issue at the Olympics but the opportunity to compete, to try, and to give one's best effort.

Regardless of the arena in which you compete, *winning* is not what is truly important. Giving your best effort to a challenge is what molds within you the lasting traits and character that are better than gold.

• •

The sluggard craves and gets nothing, but the desires of the diligent are fully satisfied.

PROVERBS 13:4 NIV

> Success is never final; failure is never fatal; it is courage that counts.

In *The Seven Habits of Highly Effective People*, Stephen R. Covey writes: "One of the most inspiring times Sandra and I have ever had took place over a four-year period with a dear friend of ours named Carol, who had a wasting cancer disease. She had been one of Sandra's bridesmaids, and they had been best friends for over 25 years.

"When Carol was in the very last stages of the disease, Sandra spent time at her bedside helping her write her personal history. She returned from those protracted and difficult sessions almost transfixed by admiration for her friend's courage and her desire to write special messages to be given to her children at different stages in their lives.

"Carol would take as little pain-killing medication as possible, so that she had full access to her mental and emotional faculties. Then she would whisper into a tape recorder or to Sandra directly as she took notes. Carol was so proactive, so brave, and so concerned about others that she became an enormous source of inspiration to many people around her."

In today's world, perhaps one trait is needed desperately. Seek to develop it. It's called *courage.*

• •

Be of good courage, and he shall strengthen your heart, all ye that hope in the LORD.

PSALM 31:24

• •

I count him braver who overcomes
his desires than him who conquers
his enemies; for the hardest
victory is the victory over self.

• •

A quiet forest dweller who lived high above
an Austrian village in the Alps was hired by a town
council to keep the pristine mountain springs—
the source of the town's water supply—clear of
debris. With faithful regularity, the old man
patrolled the hills, clearing away silt and removing
leaves and branches from the springs. Over time,
the village became prosperous. Mill wheels turned,
farms were irrigated, and tourists came. Years
passed. Then at a council meeting about the city
budget, a member noticed the salary figure for the
old man. He asked, "Who is he, and why do we
keep him on the payroll? Has anybody seen him?

For all we know, he might be dead." The council voted to dispense with his services.

For several weeks nothing changed. Then the trees began to shed their leaves. One afternoon, a town citizen noticed a brown tint to the water. Within another week, a slick covered sections of the canals, and a foul odor was detected. Sickness broke out.

The town council called a special meeting, and reversing their error in judgment, rehired the old man. Renewed life soon returned to the village as the sparkling waters returned.

Not everyone's job will make the six o'clock news every day; but no matter where God places you, do your work unto Him, and He will reward you for your faithfulness.

• •

I beat my body and make it my slave.

1 CORINTHIANS 9:27 NIV

> Vision is the world's most desperate
> need. There are no hopeless situations,
> only people who think hopelessly.

One of the great disasters of history took place in 1271. In that year, Niccolo and Matteo Polo, the father and uncle of Marco Polo, visited Kubla Khan, who was considered the world ruler, with authority over all China, all India, and all of the East.

The Kubla Khan was attracted to the story of Christianity as Niccolo and Matteo told it to him. He said to them, "You shall go to your high priest and tell him on my behalf to send me a hundred men skilled in your religion and I shall be baptized, and when I am baptized all my barons and great men will be baptized and their subjects will receive baptism, too, and so there will be more Christians here than there are in your parts."

Nothing was done, however, in response to what the Kubla Khan had requested. After thirty years, only a handful of missionaries was sent. It was too few too late.

The West apparently did not have the vision to see the East won to Christ. The mind boggles at the possible ways the world might be different today if thirteenth-century China, India, and the other areas of the Orient had been converted to Christianity.

If you lack vision today, ask God for it. He has wonders to reveal to you that you can't yet imagine!

• •

Where there is no vision,

the people perish.

PROVERBS 29:18

• •

People are lonely because they
build walls instead of bridges.

• •

A fable is told of a young orphan boy who
had no family and no one to love him. Feeling sad
and lonely, he was walking through a meadow
one day when he saw a small butterfly caught in a
thorn bush. The more the butterfly struggled to
free itself, the deeper the thorns cut into its fragile
body. The boy carefully released the butterfly, but
instead of flying away, the butterfly transformed
into an angel right before his eyes.

The boy rubbed his eyes in disbelief as the
angel said, "For your wonderful kindness, I will
do whatever you would like." The little boy
thought for a moment and then said, "I want to
be happy!" The angel replied, "Very well," and
then leaned toward him, whispered in his ear,
and vanished.

As the little boy grew up, there was no one in the land as happy as he. When people asked him the secret of his happiness, he would only smile and say, "I listened to an angel when I was a little boy."

On his deathbed, his neighbors rallied around him and asked him to divulge the key to his happiness before he died. The old man finally told them: "The angel told me that everyone, no matter how secure they seemed, no matter how old or young, how rich or poor, had need of me."

You have something to give to everyone you come in contact with today. Build bridges instead of walls!

• •

You should be like one big happy family. . . . loving one another with tender hearts and humble minds.

1 PETER 3:8 TLB

•••••••••••••••••••••••••••

Forgiveness means giving up your right to punish another.

•••••••••••••••••••••••••••

Lloyd John Ogilvie wrote in *Let God Love You*, "The hardest time to be gentle is when we know we are right and someone else is obviously dead wrong. . . . But the greatest temptation for most of us is when someone has failed us and has admitted it, and their destiny or happiness is in our hands. We hold the power to give or refuse a blessing."

"Recently, a dear friend hurt me in both word and action. Each time we met . . . I almost began to enjoy the leverage of being the offended one. His first overtures of restitution were resisted because of the gravity of the judgment I had made. He had taken a key idea I had shared with him in confidence and had developed it as his own before I had a chance to use it. The plagiarism of ideas had been coupled with the use of some of my written material, reproduced under his name. . . . The most difficult thing was to surrender my indignation and work through my hurt. . . . "

"Finally, the Lord got me where he wanted me. . . . His word to me was clear and undeniable, 'Lloyd, why is it so important to you who gets the credit, just so my work gets done?' I gave up my right to be what only God could be as this man's judge and savior. The gentle attitude began to flow."

When we withhold forgiveness, it not only hurts the person we don't want to forgive, it hurts us. Our creativity and joy in life are stifled. When we forgive, we release peace and restoration to the forgiven and to ourselves.

• •

"When you stand praying, if you hold anything against anyone, forgive him, so that your Father in heaven may forgive you your sins."

MARK 11:25 NIV

· ·

The most important single ingredient
in the formula of success is knowing
how to get along with people.

· ·

Many people today seem to go through
their day with their stingers out, ready to attack
others or to defend their position at the slightest
provocation. We all do well, however, to consider the full nature of the bees we sometimes
seem to emulate.

Bees readily feed each other, sometimes even
a bee of a different colony. The worker bees feed
the queen bee, who cannot feed herself. They
feed the drones during their period of usefulness
in the hive. They feed the young. They seem to
enjoy this social act of mutual feeding.

Bees cluster together for warmth in cold
weather and fan their wings to cool the hive in hot
weather, thus working for one another's comfort.

When the time comes for bees to move to new quarters, scouts report back to the group, doing a dance very similar to the one used to report a find of honey. When enough scouts have confirmed the suitability of the new location, the bees appear to make a common decision, take wing, and migrate together—all at the same time—in what we call a swarm.

Only as a last-resort measure of self-defense do bees engage their stingers and then, never against their fellow bees. We would do well to learn from them!

• •

See that no one pays back evil for
evil, but always try to do good to
each other and to everyone else.

1 THESSALONIANS 5:15 TLB

Everyone thinks of changing
the world, but no one
thinks of changing himself.

Andrew Carnegie, considered to be one of
the first to emphasize self-esteem and the potential for inner greatness, was famous for his ability
to produce millionaires from among his employees. One day a reporter asked him, "How do you
account for the fact you have forty-three millionaires working for you?"

Carnegie replied, "They weren't rich when
they came. We work with people the same way
you mine gold. You have to remove a lot of dirt
before you find a small amount of gold."

Andrew Carnegie knew how to bring about
change in people. He helped them realize their
hidden treasure within, inspired them to develop
it, and then watched with encouragement as their
lives were transformed.

The philosopher and psychologist William James once said, "Compared to what we ought to be, we are only half awake. We are making use of only a small part of our physical and mental resources. Stating the thing broadly, the human individual thus lives far within his limits. He possesses powers of various sorts which he habitually fails to use."

In other words, most people only develop a fraction of their abilities. Go for a bigger percentage in *your* life. Find the gold within!

• •

"Unless you change and become like little children, you will never enter the kingdom of heaven."

MATTHEW 18:3 NIV

Courage is resistance to fear, mastery of fear——not absence of fear.

Several years ago, a well-known television circus developed an act involving Bengal tigers. The act was performed live before a large audience. One night, the tiger trainer went into the cage with several tigers, and the door was routinely locked behind him. Spotlights flooded the cage, and television cameras moved in close, so the audience could see every detail as he skillfully put the tigers through their paces.

In the middle of the performance, the worst happened: the lights went out. For nearly thirty long seconds, the trainer was locked in with the tigers in the darkness. With their superb night vision, the tigers could see him, but he could not see them. Still, he survived. When the lights came back on, he calmly finished his performance.

When the trainer was asked how he felt, he admitted to feeling chilling fear at first; but then, he said, he realized that even though he couldn't see the big cats, *they didn't know he couldn't see them.* He said, "I just kept cracking my whip and talking to them until the lights came on. They never knew I couldn't see them as well as they could see me."

Keep talking back to the tigers of fear that seem to be stalking you. They will obey your voice of faith!

• •

Yea, though I walk through the valley
of the shadow of death, I will fear
no evil: for thou art with me; thy
rod and thy staff they comfort me.

PSALM 23:4

> Prayer is an invisible tool
> which is wielded in a visible world.

Both a major thoroughfare in Tel Aviv and a bridge that spans the Jordan River are named in honor of Viscount Edmund Henry Hynman Allenby, a British soldier. As commander of the Egyptian Expeditionary Forces, he outwitted and defeated the Turks in Palestine in 1917 and 1918, conquering Jerusalem without ever firing a single gun.

As a British soldier, Allenby was noncommittal about the official British policies concerning the establishment of a Jewish national home, but he did have a deep understanding of the Jews' desire to dwell in Palestine. At a reception in London, he once told how as a little boy, he had knelt to say his evening prayers, repeating with his childhood lisp the words his mother prayed: "And, O Lord, we would not forget Thine ancient people, Israel; hasten the day when Israel shall again be Thy people and shall be restored to Thy favor and to their land."

Allenby concluded, "I never knew then that God would give me the privilege of helping to answer my own childhood prayers."

What you pray today may well be part of tomorrow's work. The world you envision in prayer may well be the world in which you one day will live!

• •

The weapons of our warfare are not carnal, but mighty through God to the pulling down of strong holds.

2 CORINTHIANS 10:4

Money is like an arm or leg: use it or lose it.

A strange memorial can be found in the Mount Hope Cemetery of Hiawatha, Kansas. John M. Davis, an orphan, developed a strong dislike for his wife's family and insisted that none of his fortune go to them. He also refused requests that he eventually bequeath his estate for a hospital desperately needed in the area. Instead, after his wife died in 1930, Mr. Davis chose to invest in an elaborate tomb for himself and his wife. The tomb includes a number of statues depicting the couple at various stages of their lives. One statue is of Mr. Davis as a lonely man seated beside an empty chair. It is titled "the vacant chair." Another shows him placing a wreath in front of his wife's tombstone. Many of the statues are made of Kansas granite. No money was left for the memorial's upkeep.

Today, largely because of its weight, this costly memorial is slowly sinking into the ground. It has become weathered and worn from the strong winds in this plains state. The townspeople regard the Davis tomb as an "old man's folly;" and many predict that within the next fifty years, the memorial will have become obliterated beyond recognition and will need to be demolished. What could have been a living legacy will eventually become granite dust.

The Bible encourages us many times not to hoard up money to be used for our own selfish desires but to be kind to the poor. When we do so, God blesses us with more. The more we give, the more we receive; and our legacy will last well into the future instead of sinking into oblivion.

• •

"To him who has will more be given . . . and he will have great plenty; but from him who has not, even the little he has will be taken away."

MATTHEW 13:12 TLB

• 283 •

In trying times, don't quit trying.

In 1894, a sixteen-year-old found this note from his rhetoric teacher at Harrow, in England, attached to his report card: "A conspicuous lack of success." The young man kept on trying and went on to become one of the most famous speakers of the twentieth century. His name was Winston Churchill.

In 1902, an aspiring twenty-eight-year-old writer received a rejection letter from the poetry editor of the *Atlantic Monthly*. Returned, with a batch of poems he had sent, was this curt note: "Our magazine has no room for your vigorous verse." He kept on trying, however, and went on to see his work published. The poet's name was Robert Frost.

In 1905, the University of Bern turned down a Ph.D. dissertation as being fanciful and irrelevant. The young physics student who wrote the dissertation kept on trying and went on to develop some of his ideas into widely accepted theories. His name was Albert Einstein.

When rejection shakes your resolve and dims your goals, keep on trying. If you do not quit, one day, you will be living out your dreams!

• •

The righteous also shall hold on his way, and he that hath clean hands shall be stronger and stronger.

JOB 17:9

Let us not say, "Every man is the architect of his own fortune;" but let us say, "Every man is the architect of his own character."

When Chief Justice Charles Evans Hughes moved to Washington, D.C., to take up his duties on the Supreme Court, he transferred his church membership letter to a Baptist church in the area.

It was customary for all new members in this church to come to the front of the sanctuary at the close of the worship service, so they might be officially introduced and welcomed. The first person to be called forward that morning was Ah Sing, a Chinese laundryman who had moved to Washington from the West Coast. He took his place at the far side of the church. As the dozen or so others were called forward that day, they came forward and stood on the opposite side of the church, leaving Ah Sing standing alone.

Finally Chief Justice Hughes was called forward, and he immediately made his way to the front and proceeded to stand next to Ah Sing. The minister who welcomed the group into church fellowship said, "I do not want this congregation to miss this remarkable illustration of the fact that at the cross of Jesus Christ, the ground is level."

Your character is shown in many ways, but one of the most obvious is the way you treat people. You will grow in character and reputation if you treat others with kindness.

• •

Till I die I will not remove mine integrity
from me. My righteousness I hold fast,
and will not let it go: my heart shall
not reproach me so long as I live.

JOB 27:5–6

It is impossible for that man
to despair who remembers
that his Helper is omnipotent.

E. Stanley Jones tells the story of a missionary who became lost in an African jungle. Looking around, he saw nothing but bush and a few clearings. He stumbled about until he finally came across a native hut. He asked one of the natives if he could lead him out of the jungle and back to the mission station. The native agreed to help him.

"Thank you!" exclaimed the missionary. "Which way do I go?" The native replied, "Walk." And so they did, hacking their way through the unmarked jungle for more than an hour.

In pausing to rest, the missionary looked around and had the same overwhelming sense that he was lost. Again, all he could see was bush and a few clearings. "Are you quite sure this is the way?" he asked. "I don't see any path."

The native looked at him and replied, "Bwana, in this place there is no path. I am the path."

When we have no clues about which direction we're going, we must remember that God who guides us is omniscient—all wise. When we run out of time, we must remember that God is omnipresent—all time is in His hand. When we are weak, we must remember that God is omnipotent—all-powerful. He is everything we need.

● ●

I will lift up my eyes to the mountains;
From where shall my help come? My help comes
from the LORD, Who made heaven and earth.

PSALM 121:1–2 NASB

. . . .

Service is nothing but
love in work clothes.

. . . .

Lord of all pots and pans and things,
Since I've no time to be
A saint by doing lovely things,
Or watching late with Thee,
Or dreaming in the dawnlight,
Or storming heaven's gates,
Make me a saint by getting meals,
And washing up the plates.
Although I have Martha's hands,
I have a Mary's mind;
And when I black the boots and shoes,
Thy sandals, Lord, I find.
I think of how they trod the earth,
Each time I scrub the floor.
Accept this meditation, Lord,
I haven't time for more.
Warm all the kitchen with Thy love,

And light it with Thy peace;
Forgive me all my worrying,
And make all grumbling cease.
Thou who didst love to give men food,
In a room or by the sea,
Accept this service that I do—
I do it unto Thee.

—Unknown

• •

"The more lowly your service
to others, the greater you are.
To be the greatest, be a servant."

MATTHEW 23:11 TLB

Those that have done nothing
in life are not qualified to
judge those that have done little.

In the 1700s, an English cobbler kept a map
of the world on his workshop wall so that he
might be reminded to pray for the nations of the
world. As the result of such prayer, he became
especially burdened for a specific missionary out-
reach. He shared this burden at a meeting of
ministers but was told by a senior minister,
"Young man, sit down. When God wants to
convert the heathen, He will do it without your
help or mine."

The cobbler, William Carey, did not let this
man's remarks put out the flame of his concern.
When he couldn't find others to support the missionary cause that had burdened his soul, he
became a missionary himself. His pioneering

efforts in India are legendary; his mighty exploits for God are recorded by many church historians.

Be careful how you respond to the enthusiasm of others. Don't dampen someone's zeal for God. Be cautious in how you respond to the new ideas of another, that you don't squelch their God-given creativity.

Be generous and kind in evaluating the work of others so that you might encourage those things which are worthy. Be slow to judge and quick to praise. Then pray for the same in your own life!

● ●

Judge not, and ye shall not be judged:
condemn not, and ye shall not be condemned.

LUKE 6:37

People, places, and things were never
meant to give us life. God alone
is the author of a fulfilling life.

A young man once came to Jesus, asking
Him what he needed to do to have eternal life.
Jesus replied that he should keep the commandments. The young man then claimed that he had
always kept them. Jesus advised, *If you would be
perfect, sell everything you have, give the money to
the poor, and come and follow me (Matthew 19:21).*

The Scriptures tell us that the young man
*went away sorrowful: for he had great possessions
(v. 22).* The young man not only had great possessions, but apparently those possessions had
him! He couldn't bear to part with earthly, temporary goods in order to obtain heavenly, eternal
goods. Jesus also taught, of course, that Heaven's
wealth can be ours now. This young man didn't
have to wait until he died to attain the benefits of

eternal life. If he had been willing to give up his hold on his stuff, he could have enjoyed great joy, peace, and fulfillment in life—things he was apparently lacking or he wouldn't have asked Jesus the question.

Take a look at your possessions today. Are there books, tapes, or clothes you can give away to someone in need of learning, inspiration, or clothing? Discover how rewarding giving can be!

• •

I am come that they might have life, and that they might have it more abundantly.

JOHN 10:10

> One man with courage
> makes a majority.

A teenager named Buck was walking to his father's apartment from a subway stop one day when he suddenly realized that two men were flanking him.

"Give me your wallet," one of the men insisted. "I have a gun. Give me your wallet, or I'll shoot."

"No," Buck said.

"Hey, man, you don't understand. We're robbing you. Give me your wallet."

"No."

"Give me your wallet, or I'll knife you."

"No."

"Give me your wallet, or we'll beat you up."

By now the robber was pleading more than he was demanding.

"No," Buck said once again. He kept walking, and a few steps later, he realized that the two men had disappeared. As he related this story to a friend, the friend asked, "Weren't you scared?"

Buck replied, "Of course I was scared!"

"Then why didn't you give them your wallet?"

"Because," Buck answered matter-of-factly, "My learner's permit is in it."

While it may be wise to give in to the demands of a thief, the first and best answer to fear is always no!

• •

Be strong and of a good courage . . .
for the LORD thy God . . . will not
fail thee, nor forsake thee.

DEUTERONOMY 31:6

· ·

You will never make a more important decision than the person you marry.

· ·

When Ruth Bell was a teenager, she was sent from her childhood home in China to school in Korea. At the time, she fully intended to follow in her parents' footsteps and become a missionary. She envisioned herself a confirmed old maid, ministering to the people of Tibet. While at school, however, Ruth did give some serious thought to the kind of husband that she *might* consider. As she tells in her book *A Time for Remembering,* she listed these particulars:

"If I marry: He must be so tall that when he is on his knees, as one has said, he reaches all the way to heaven. His shoulders must be broad enough to bear the burden of a family. His lips must be strong enough to smile, firm enough to say no, and tender enough to kiss. Love must be so deep that it takes its stand in Christ and so wide that it takes the whole lost world in. He must be active enough to save souls. He must be big enough to be gentle and great enough to be thoughtful. His arms must be strong enough to carry a little child."

Ruth Bell never did become a full-time missionary in Tibet. She did, however, find a man worth marrying—Billy Graham. As his wife, Ruth Bell Graham became a missionary to the whole world!

Your spouse will be the most important person in your life. It's crucial to marry the right person. Think about the qualities that you would like to have in a mate. If you haven't already, begin to pray for the person you will eventually marry. Even if you haven't met him or her yet, God knows who he or she is.

• •

Therefore shall a man leave his father
and his mother, and shall cleave unto
his wife: and they shall be one flesh.

GENESIS 2:24

························

The Bible has a word to describe
"safe" sex: it's called marriage.

························

The 1960s were known for many rebellions,
among them the sexual revolution. Free love
spilled from the hippie movement into the main-
stream American culture. Premarital sexual relations sanctioned by the new morality became
openly flaunted.

One of the unexpected results of this trend,
however, received little publicity. As reported by
Dr. Francis Braceland, past president of the
American Psychiatric Association and editor of
the *American Journal of Psychiatry,* an increasing
number of young people were admitted to
mental hospitals during that time. In discussing
this finding at a National Methodist Convocation
of Medicine and Theology, Braceland concluded,
"A more lenient attitude on campus about premarital sexual experience has imposed stresses on

some college women severe enough to cause emotional breakdown."

Looking back over the years since the new morality was sanctioned by a high percentage of the American culture, one finds a rising number of rapes, abortions, divorces, premarital pregnancies, single-family homes, and cases of sexually transmitted diseases, including herpes and HIV.

The evidence is compelling: the old morality produced safer, healthier, and happier people!

• •

Marriage should be honored by all, and the marriage bed kept pure, for God will judge the adulterer and all the sexually immoral.

HEBREWS 13:4 NIV

Nothing is ever lost by courtesy. . . .
It pleases him who gives and
him who receives, and thus,
like mercy, it is twice blessed.

We often refer to courtesy as "common courtesy," but it is far from common these days. In fact, it is pretty rare. How many people do you know who follow the basic common courtesies given in this section?

A father once remarked about his three children: "My children may not be the brightest children in their class. They may not be the most talented or the most skilled. They may not achieve great fame or earn millions of dollars. But by my insisting that they have good manners, I know they will be welcome in all places and by all people." How true!

Good manners—exhibiting common courtesies—are like a calling card. They open doors that are otherwise shut to those who are rude, crude, or unmannerly. They bring welcome invitations and quite often, return engagements. They cover a multitude of weaknesses and flaws. They make other people feel good about themselves, and they in turn, extend kindness and generosity they might not otherwise exhibit. Good manners are a prerequisite for good friendships, good business associations, and good marriages. They are the key to success!

• •

While we have opportunity,

let us do good to all people.

GALATIANS 6:10 NASB

Two Incredibly Powerful Words:
"Thank You."

Which virtuous behaviors on earth will still be required in Heaven?

Courage? No. There will be nothing to fear in Heaven. Hope? No. We will have all that we desire.

Faith? No. We will be in the presence of the Source of our faith, and all those things for which we have believed will have their fulfillment in Him and by His hand.

Acts of charity toward those in need? No. There will be no hunger, thirst, nakedness, or homelessness in Heaven. All needs will be supplied.

Sympathy? No, for there will be no more tears and no more pain.

Kindness and gratitude? Yes! There will still be room for showing kindness to others, for being grateful for the kindnesses others have shown us.

Kindness puts people at ease, which in turn makes them more cooperative and happy. Immanuel Kant once said, "Always treat a human being as a person, that is, as an end in himself, and not merely as a means to your end." Strive to impart dignity and self-worth to all you meet. Consider it dress rehearsal for your future life in Heaven!

• •

"Treat others the same way
you want them to treat you."

LUKE 6:31 NASB

Children who bring honor
to their parents reap
blessings from their God.

A mother watched with raised eyebrows as her two sons took a hammer and a few nails from the kitchen utility drawer and scurried to one of the boys' rooms, giggling and talking in low voices. When she didn't hear any hammering, she continued with her chores. Then from the kitchen window, she saw one of the boys take a stepladder from the garage. He disappeared from sight before she could call to him. A few minutes later her other son came into the kitchen to ask if she had any rope. "No," Mom said. "What's going on?" Her son said, "Nothin'." Mom pressed, "Are you sure?" But her son was out of sight.

Highly suspicious, Mom went to her son's room. She found the door closed and locked. She knocked. "What are you boys doing in there?" she asked. One son replied, "Nothin'." Suspecting great mischief, she demanded entrance. "I want you to open this door right now!" she said. A few seconds later, the door popped open, and her son shouted, "Surprise!" as he handed her a rather crudely wrapped present. "Happy birthday, Mom!" the other boy added. Truly surprised, the mother stammered, "But what about the hammer, nails, ladder, and rope?" The boys grinned, "Those were just decoys, Mom."

• •

Honor your father and your mother,
so that you may live long in the land
the LORD your God is giving you.

EXODUS 20:12 NIV

• 307 •

> Those who desire to lead
> must first learn to respect
> authority and obey.

While driving down a country road, a man came to a very narrow bridge. In front of the bridge, there was a sign that read, "Yield." Seeing no oncoming cars, the man continued across the bridge and to his destination. On his way back this same route, he came to the same one-lane bridge, now from the opposite direction. To his surprise, he saw another "Yield" sign posted there.

Curious, he thought, *I'm sure there was one positioned on the other side.* Sure enough, when he reached the other side of the bridge and looked back, he saw the sign. Yield signs had been placed at both ends of the bridge, obviously with the intent that drivers from both directions were requested to give each other the right-of-way. It was a reasonable and doubly sure way to prevent a head-on collision.

If you find yourself in a combative situation with someone who has more authority than you—or equal authority—it is always wise to yield to them. If they indeed have more authority, a lack of submission will put you in a position to be punished or reprimanded. If you are of equal authority, an exercise of your power will only build resentment in a person better kept as an ally. As the Bible says, we are to *prefer one another (Romans 12:10).*

● ●

Show respect for everyone. Love Christians everywhere. Fear God and honor the government.

1 PETER 2:17 TLB

He who created us without
our help will not save us
without our consent.

The letters RSVP stand for the French phrase *répondéz s'il vous plaît* . . . or, "please respond." This phrase on an invitation asks that you let the host or hostess know whether you plan to attend the function. Every invitation marked with rsvp requires that you call or write the host to let them know that you either will or will not be there.

Occasionally, a handwritten invitation will say, "RSVP, regrets only." In this case, you are required to notify the host only if you will *not* be attending. A truly thoughtful guest who plans to attend, however, will call or mail a note to the host to thank them for the invitation and to confirm that he or she will attend.

Imagine that you planned a catered party for fifty guests and you were paying twenty-five dollars per guest. Then imagine that half your guests failed to respond, and ten of them did not show up. You would be spending two hundred and fifty dollars for people who simply were not considerate enough to let you know that they could not be present. Would you consider those people to be thoughtful friends?

The most important RSVP in all of life is our response to God's invitation to spend eternity with Him in Heaven. Have you sent your RSVP?

• •

If you confess with your mouth, "Jesus is Lord," and believe in your heart that God raised him from the dead, you will be saved.

ROMANS 10:9 NIV

• •

Before you borrow money from a friend,
decide which you need more.

• •

A store once had this layaway policy: "We
hold it in the store while you pay for it. You're
mad. You take it from the store, and you don't
pay for it. We're mad. Better that you're mad."
Mark Twain's neighbor may have had this policy
in mind when Twain asked to borrow a certain
book he had spotted in his neighbor's library.
"Why, yes, Mr. Clemens, you're more than
welcome to it," the neighbor said. "But I must ask
you to read it here. You know I make it a rule
never to let any book go out of my library."

Several days later, the neighbor came to
Twain's house and asked if he could borrow his
lawn mower since his had been taken to the
repair shop. "Why, certainly," the humorist
replied. "You're more than welcome to it. But I

must ask you to use it only in my yard. You know I make it a rule."

Treat what you borrow as if it were a prized possession, returning it promptly. If something happens to it while it is in your possession, make repairs or replace it—not to your satisfaction but to the satisfaction of the owner. Always remember, while the item is in your hands, it is not yours. It still belongs to the other person.

• •

If a man borrows an animal from his neighbor
and it is injured or dies while the owner
is not present, he must make restitution.

EXODUS 22:14 NIV

God has given man one tongue
but two ears that we may hear
twice as much as we speak.

M r. Brown was in his final year of semi-
nary, preparing to become a pastor. The policy of
his school called for him to be available at a
moment's notice to fill in for local churches who
might need a preacher. Mr. Brown eagerly
awaited such an opportunity, and at long last, his
moment arrived. The pastor of a country church
was called away on an emergency, and Mr. Brown
was asked to fill the pulpit.

Having waited so long for the opportunity
and having so much to say, Mr. Brown soon
became completely immersed in his own words.
The more he preached, the more he became
inspired to preach. When he glanced at his watch,
he was shocked to see that he had preached for a
full hour. He was truly embarrassed since he had

been allotted only thirty minutes to preach. Knowing that he had preached well into the lunch hour, he made a heartfelt apology to the congregation and sat down.

A young woman hurried to him after the service ended. Obviously more impressed with his personality and appearance—and perhaps his availability—than she was with his message, she gushed, "Oh, Brother Brown, you needn't have apologized. You really didn't talk long—it just seemed long."

The old rule of thumb is, "Always leave them wanting more."

• •

Do not keep talking so proudly or
let your mouth speak such arrogance.

1 SAMUEL 2:3 NIV

• •

Work without a vision is drudgery; a
vision without work is only a dream;
work with a vision is victory.

• •

Helen Keller overcame the most difficult of
physical challenges to become one of the greatest
Americans of the twentieth century. As the result
of a fever when she was a baby, Helen was left
deaf, blind, and unable to speak. Eventually, with
dedication, she learned to communicate with
Braille; and her life became an inspiration for
millions of people, including Mark Twain, an
ardent admirer. She was invited to visit every U.S.
president during her lifetime.

As a teenager, she struggled to achieve, finally
graduating with honors from Radcliffe College.
She wrote numerous articles, gave lectures for the
American Foundation for the Blind, and raised
more than two million dollars for the foundation's work. On her eightieth birthday, the

American Foundation for Overseas Blind
honored her by announcing the Helen Keller
International Award for those who give outstanding help to the blind.

Sometimes as young adults, we think there
are too many strikes against us—our lives are just
too hard. Yet Helen rose above her limitations to
make a lasting contribution to our society. Not
only are we called to overcome our faults and
weaknesses, but we are asked to exercise our
strengths. We are challenged to do more than just
survive in this world. God desires that we set our
minds, hearts, and energy to the work He has
planned for us. He's given you the talent to make
your dreams a reality.

• •

Work hard so God can say to you, "Well done."

Be a good workman, one who does not need

to be ashamed when God examines your work.

2 TIMOTHY 2:15 TLB

Acknowledgments

We acknowledge and thank the following people for the quotes used in this book: Syrus (10, 200), Ralph Waldo Emerson (12, 58, 160), Jim Patrick (16), Harry Emerson Fosdick (18, 204), Calvin Coolidge (20, 210), Sprat (26), Les Brown (28), John D. Rockefeller Jr. (30), Dr. Eugene Swearingen (32, 36, 298), Thomas Jefferson (34, 116), Robert C. Edward (38), Ed Cole (40, 64, 280), Arnold Glasow (42), Kin Hubbard (48), Henry Ward Beecher (50, 246), John A. Shedd (54, 74), Dwight L. Moody (60, 88), H.E. Jansen (66), Roy Disney (76), Descartes (78), Helen Keller (80), Seneca (82), Aristotle (84, 162, 266), William A. Ward (90), Charles H. Spurgeon (92, 124), Moliére (96), Bob Bales (98), Solon (100), Charles C. Noble (102), Samuel Johnson (104, 292), Eleanor Roosevelt (106), John Sculley (108), George Bernard Shaw (110), Oprah Winfrey (112), Benjamin Franklin (120, 224), Woodrow Wilson (122), William Lyon Phelps (126), Washington Irving (128), Terence (132), Henry Wadsworth Longfellow (144), Josh Billings (146), Jean Paul Richter (150), William James (152), Samuel Butler (154), H.P. Liddon (156), George Elliot (158), John R. Rice (164), William H. Danforth (166, 186, 220), Thomas A. Edison (168), Orlando A. Battista (170, 202), George Edward Woodberry (172), Ronald